The
ECONOMY OF GOD
AND THE
MYSTERY
OF THE
TRANSMISSION
OF THE
DIVINE TRINITY

WITNESS LEE

Living Stream Ministry
Anaheim, California

First Edition, August 2001.

ISBN 0-7363-0851-2

Published by

Living Stream Ministry
2431 W. La Palma Ave., Anaheim, CA 92801 U.S.A.
P. O. Box 2121, Anaheim, CA 92814 U.S.A.

Printed in the United States of America

01 02 03 04 05 06 07 / 10 9 8 7 6 5 4 3 2 1

CONTENTS

PREFACE

This book is composed of messages given by Brother Witness Lee from March through June of 1986 in the full-time training in Taipei, Taiwan.

The first three chapters give a general discussion of four great matters in the Bible: the economy of God, the dispensing of God, the union of God with His believers, and the corporate expression of God. The subsequent chapters go on to explain the profound truths and the experience of life related to these four great matters according to the book of Ephesians, the Gospel of John, and the Gospel of Matthew. Following this, the book proceeds to offer guidance to all those who have a heart to serve the Lord full time concerning the building up of themselves in the matters of life, truth, character, learning languages, knowing the church, living a healthy life, and managing personal finances as living witnesses of the Lord, so that they may become useful vessels in the Lord's hands.

Although this series of messages was released in the full-time training, the speaking concerning the economy of God and the mystery of the transmission of the Divine Trinity, as well as the words of earnest instruction to the full-time serving ones concerning life, truth, character, living, and finances are topics and lessons intimately related to all of the children of God today. Hence, this book is necessary reading for all of us!

The Editorial Section
Taiwan Gospel Book Room
August 20, 1998

CHAPTER ONE

KNOWING THE ECONOMY OF GOD

A follower of the Lord must be a pursuer, and there are at least a few things that he must pursue throughout his entire life: life, truth, the filling of the Holy Spirit, character training, and the knowledge of God's eternal economy.

PURSUING LIFE

First of all, a follower of the Lord must pursue the growth in the divine life by passing through the processes of sanctification, renewing, transformation, and conformation until he reaches the stages of maturity and glorification.

PURSUING TRUTH

Second, a follower of the Lord must pursue the full knowledge of the truth. Throughout the six thousand years of human history there have been countless writings of significant value in various fields, such as philosophy, science, and religion. Up to this day, however, in the whole world every person of integrity and fair-mindedness—whether he is a God-fearing person or an atheist, a Christian or a non-Christian—recognizes that the Bible is the most outstanding and profound book in human culture. The Bible, composed of sixty-six books, was written in various places (both Jewish and Gentile) by more than forty authors over a period of one thousand and six hundred years. In spite of this, the Bible is a complete book with a beginning and an end. It begins with God's creation and concludes with the New Jerusalem in the new heaven and new earth. Moreover, it has a final warning which says that no one should either add anything or take away anything from the Word of God (Rev 22:18-19). Anyone who takes away any words from the Bible will lose the blessings of the eternal life of God—that person will have no share of the tree of life, the river of water of life, and the holy city. This punishment will be meted out to those who take away anything from the words of the Bible. Those who add something to the words of the Bible will also suffer the punishment of God's eternal judgment, which is mainly to perish in the lake of fire. Hence, the Bible has an eternal beginning and an eternal ending.

Throughout the centuries innumerable Biblical scholars have studied the Bible according to the Hebrew language of the Old Testament and the Greek language of the New Testament by expending their energy over their entire lifetime and by using all the methods of their wisdom. However, up to the present no one has ever been able to claim that he has thoroughly studied the Bible. This shows that the Bible is truly mysterious. Hence, in addition to the ones who serve God full time for their whole life, even those who merely have a desire to follow the Lord faithfully must do their best to study and know the Bible.

When we studied in school, we spent a great deal of our effort to get into every subject thoroughly. However, I cannot find the proper words to express what kind of effort, energy, wisdom, knowledge, and understanding is needed for the study of the Bible. From what I have personally experienced in this matter, I can only affirm that I cannot express with human language what kind of effort and how much time we have to devote to the study of the Bible.

The division of the sections of the Bible is of profound significance, and even the arrangement of the books of the Bible inspires admiration. For example, according to the natural concept of the Chinese, who are particularly fond of maxims and mottoes, it would be best to have the book of Proverbs at the beginning of the Bible. However, the first book of the Bible is not Leviticus, still less Proverbs, the favorite book of the Chinese, but Genesis; moreover, the last book of the Bible is neither Matthew nor Isaiah but Revelation. If the sequence of the Bible were arranged according to man's natural concept, then the proper significance would be lost. Therefore, the order of the books of the Bible has profound significance.

The chapters of each book of the Scriptures are also divinely arranged. The things that are stated explicitly, of course, have profound significance; however, certain things that are not mentioned are even more profound in their significance. For instance, Genesis 14 tells us that when Abraham returned after winning a battle, Melchisedec, the king of Salem, the priest of the Most High God, went to meet him, ministered bread and wine to him, and blessed him (vv. 17-19). Strangely, however, Genesis does not tell us anything about the origin of Melchisedec. According to the style of Genesis, whenever someone is mentioned, there is usually an account of his background. For example, there are clear records of the backgrounds of people such as Adam and Noah to let us know of whom they were born, what their accomplishments were, and how long they lived. However, the record in Genesis concerning Melchisedec does not disclose to us his beginning or his end. Therefore, we do not know where he came from or where he went.

In Hebrews 7, however, Paul tells us that Melchisedec, who was a type of Christ as the eternal Son of God, had no father, no mother, no genealogy, no beginning of days, and no end of life (v. 3). This shows us the reason why the record of his background was omitted in Genesis. Of course, Melchisedec could not actually be without parents, as if he simply dropped from heaven, but these facts were omitted intentionally in Genesis. Even Moses, when he wrote Genesis, probably did not know why the Holy Spirit did not reveal to him the background of Melchisedec, including his birth and his death. I do not believe that Moses knew that one day Paul would use Melchisedec to typify Christ, who has no beginning, no ending, no birth, and no death. This proves that Moses wrote Genesis under the leading of the Holy Spirit.

Let us take the four Gospels as another example. The four Gospels give us a portrait of the Lord Jesus in four different aspects. However, a case may be mentioned in one book but not recorded in the other three books, while another case may be recorded in two or three books, and yet the emphasis in each of these books may be different. For example, in the case of the Lord Jesus' feeding five thousand with five loaves and two fish, the writing style of John chapter six is totally different from that of the other three Gospels. Therefore, in order to understand the full significance of any case recorded in the four Gospels, we need to study the four Gospels together and take care of every aspect of that case. Only then will we be able to have a thorough understanding and comprehension. It is surely meaningful that a certain case is recorded in some places, but it is equally meaningful, from another viewpoint, that it is omitted in other places.

In Matthew 5:18 the Lord Jesus says, "For truly I say to you, Until heaven and earth pass away, one iota or one serif shall by no means pass away from the law until all come to pass." Therefore, we who love and pursue the Lord should devote a major part of our lifetime to the study of the Bible. It is absolutely impossible to study the Bible thoroughly. We all know that our diet is of utmost importance to our health. We should pay attention not only to how much we eat but also to how properly we eat. The Cantonese, who are very particular about their eating, eat seven times a day. As followers of the Lord, we need to read the Bible every day and if possible seven times a day. You should never think that you do not need to read the Bible anymore because you have already read through it several times and have read it thoroughly. The Bible is exceedingly rich. Therefore, no matter how thoroughly you have studied it, there are still some items that you have not yet uncovered. I hope that you will not only remember this point but also practice accordingly. If you spend time to study the Bible diligently, you may wear out a Bible in seven or eight years. Your Bible will become worn out because you have studied it so diligently and so frequently. You may consider yourself to have exerted sufficient effort only after you have worn out several copies of the Bible.

The amount of effort you have put into the study of the Bible can be seen in two things. The first thing is how old your Bible is and how worn out it is. If it has not been handled often enough and is still very clean, preserved intact, and kept in the same place, this proves that you have not spent time to study it. The second thing is how many circles, dots, and lines there are in your Bible, how many different colors there are, and how many annotations have been written in it. This does not mean that you should draw or write indiscriminately. The circles, dots, and lines you draw, the colors you apply, and the words you write must all be meaningful, and the more the better.

One thing that has been a concern to me and that I have always greatly regretted is that I lost my first Bible. I truly hope that I will be able to get back that Bible because it means a great deal to me. If today someone would offer a high price to buy my old Bibles, I definitely would not sell them. To me, they are my best savings, my priceless treasures. I say this with the hope that all of you will spend time to study the Bible diligently.

PURSUING THE FILLING OF THE HOLY SPIRIT

Third, we need to be filled with the Holy Spirit daily, to "buy oil" every day. Matthew 25:1-10 clearly tells us the significance of buying oil. Many readers of the Bible know how rich the meaning of the word *buy* is. It includes confession of sins, prayer, dealing with negative things, obedience, paying the price, and following the leading of the Holy Spirit.

Being filled with the Holy Spirit is related to pursuing the growth in life. Without being filled with the Holy Spirit, it is impossible to pursue the growth in life—the growth in life is simply unattainable. Our growth in life is altogether determined by the measure of the filling of the Holy Spirit within us. The infilling of the Holy Spirit fosters the growth in life. Without being filled with the Holy Spirit, a follower of the Lord is just like a plant without soil, water, sunlight, and air; even if he lives, he is merely prolonging his life temporarily. In biblical figures, we are God's plants (cf. 1 Cor. 3:6; Col. 2:7), and the Triune God is our soil (cf. Col. 2:7), sunlight (Mal. 4:2; Luke 1:78), air (Ezek. 37:9-10, 14a; John 20:22), and water, including rain (Exo. 17:6; 1 Cor. 10:4; John 4:10, 14; 7:38-39; Rev. 22:1; cf. Gen. 2:5; Deut. 11:14; Joel 2:23, 28-29; Hosea 6:3; Zech. 10:1; Acts 2:16-18). The Holy Spirit is the processed and consummated Triune God; therefore, to be filled with the Holy Spirit is to be filled with the Triune God. When we are filled with the Triune God, we have soil, water, sunlight, and air, and the result is that we grow and become full-grown in life. We cannot say that because we were thoroughly filled with the Holy Spirit yesterday, we do not need to be filled today. We need to buy oil daily; that is, we need to experience the infilling of the Holy Spirit every day.

In the Philippines, the wind from March to May is very humid. Thus, a person easily gets sick if he is exposed to the wind. The local people prevent all kinds of illnesses by taking showers, at least once daily. People who live in the north do not need to shower every day, but if they go to the Philippines they have to take a shower daily, and each time they must shower until they are thoroughly wet. They cannot say that they do not need a shower today because they already took one yesterday. Sometimes they may even need to take a shower three times a day. This is a good illustration of being filled with the Holy Spirit. We have to be filled with the Holy Spirit every day, and every time we have to be filled through and through. Sometimes we should be filled even three times a day. We surely have to exercise ourselves seriously in these three matters: growing in life, pursuing the truth, and being filled with the Holy Spirit.

PURSUING CHARACTER TRAINING

The fourth and most important point is the training of our character. Why is character training so important? It is because the result of our pursuit in the preceding three matters depends entirely on the extent of our character training.

Character Being Related to Transformation

Character is a common term, but the training of a Christian's character is related to the transformation referred to in the Bible. The real character training of a Christian is accomplished not by outward improvement but by inward transformation. This means that although you were not born this way, after a certain kind of element has been added into you and has been mingled with you, you become different, and thus your character is changed.

Transformation Requiring Breaking

There was a certain kind of sculpture in the ancient times which was made by grinding stones into powder, adding a cementing element to the powder, and then putting the compound into a mold until it solidified into a statue. This process may be used in a limited way to describe transformation. In the process of transformation we are ground into powder and mingled with the element of the Holy Spirit. Then we are put into the death of the Lord Jesus on the cross to be pressed and shaped. Eventually our original form is changed, and what comes out is a transformed character. As fallen human beings, we inherited Adam's fallen nature. Hence, our human character, which comes out of our natural being, whether good or bad, is fallen. The unbelievers call the cultivation of character "the nurturing of human nature." History shows that people who nurture their humanity are strong in their will and able to exercise self-restraint. They develop a certain kind of character by their self-control. We Christians, however, are not like that. Our Christian character is cultivated in the death of the Lord Jesus by the breaking of the life of our old creation and the addition of the element of the Holy Spirit.

For this reason Paul said in 2 Corinthians 4 that our outer man is decaying day by day (v. 16). It is better to translate *decaying* into *being consumed, being wasted away,* or *being worn out.* In our daily living, God is continually doing in us the work of consuming, wasting away, and wearing out through His hand, or through the environment, in order to break us. *Breaking* is a fitting word because it indicates that we should not remain whole. Those who are whole cannot be transformed. Mineralogists know that diamonds are transformed from carbon that has undergone high heat and intense pressure underneath the earth for hundreds and thousands of years. All precious stones are formed in the same way; that is, they are transformed from natural substances that have gone through breaking, high temperature, and great pressure. In the same principle, if we desire to be transformed into precious stones, we also must pass through the same process and procedure.

Moreover, Paul said, "We who are alive are always being delivered unto death for Jesus' sake" (v. 11). God works in us continually to break and consume us in order to grind us into powder. We already have the life of the Lord Jesus in us; however, if we remain intact, there is no way for this life to be mingled with us. No element, regardless of what it is, can be mingled with a whole piece of stone. Thus, in order to be mingled with the life of the Lord, we must be broken and crushed. Once we are broken, the element of the Holy Spirit can be added into us and be mingled with us. Then God will also raise up the environment as high temperature and intense pressure in order to transform us into precious stones.

The Way for God to Break Us

Marriage is God's ordination. If a man or a woman is still not married after having passed the right age for marriage, there is great pressure upon them. Yet after they are married, their spouse also becomes a pressure. Without having to learn, every husband knows by nature how to wear down his wife. Likewise, without having to learn, every wife knows by nature how to give her husband a hard time. Someone may be altogether unmanageable, but once he sees his wife, he becomes just like a mouse coming face to face with a cat. Marriage life is a consuming life. Being married and yet not being consumed is an impossibility. Why are there divorces? It is because some people give up on marriage life, unable to endure the sufferings any longer. Sixty years ago when I was still young, an older person told me that marriage life is a "yoke." As soon as a person gets married, he is "yoked" and "shackled." Then, is marriage good or bad? Actually, marriage is very good because it is sovereignly arranged by God for our transformation. It is impossible to be transformed without first being ground.

The same is true in the matter of bearing children. If a woman has no child after she has been married three years, she is under a great deal of pressure to have children. However, once she gives birth to a child, the child becomes an additional pressure. A certain sister may be very difficult to deal with. Before she is married, her parents do not know how to deal with her, and after she is married, her husband does not know how to deal with her either. However, after she gives birth to a difficult child, she will be consumed and softened. Regardless of how strong or stubborn you are, God has a way to break you and transform you. After seeing others being worn down by their children, a sister once said, "I do not believe it is that hard. Wait till I have a child; I will discipline him and make him an obedient child." Eventually, after having her own child, she was even more helpless than the others. You can call the police when your house has been burglarized. However, if your children are disobedient, do you also call the police? No! You are afraid even to tell your neighbors or relatives. Our children are the most capable of wearing us out. The wives who wear out their husbands and the husbands who wear out their wives are not as skillful as the children who wear out their parents. The children's skillful wearing-out tactics really consume the parents.

Hence, from this viewpoint, character is not cultivated by having a strong will or by ill-treating the body. Rather, character is the issue of transformation in our pursuing of the Lord. Because we love the Lord, God arranges our marriage and our family in such a way so that we can be broken and be transformed.

Furthermore, the church life with all the brothers and sisters also consumes us. As humans, we have to be Christians; if we are not, we will end up in the lake of fire. However, after we become Christians, we have to live the church life. Many people acknowledge that in the church life we experience five flavors—sweet, sour, bitter, pungent, and salty—which are all for our breaking and termination. If we are still not broken, there will be high heat and great pressure to grind and crush us. Sometimes the elders grind us every day just like millstones. While the unbelievers only have a human family, we have two families: a human family and a divine family. Furthermore, both families are "yokes" and "shackles" to us, so there is no way for us to escape. If someone is tired of his job, he can either resign or endure until he retires. However, the family "yoke" and "shackle" will cease only at death. This is God's ordination; it is not decided by us but arranged by God. Therefore, Romans 8:28 says, "We know that all things work together for good to those who love God." God arranges all things to work together in order to break us, press us, and grind us into powder for our transformation.

We all know that according to God's eternal purpose we cannot run away from God. In His eternal plan with His foreknowledge and in His wisdom, God chose us before the foundation of the world. Then according to His plan we were born in this age, we grew up, we were called, and now we live the church life. Because we are constrained by God through the environment, it seems that we have no alternative but to take this way. However, in reality, if we walk on this way willingly, we will be blessed by God. Even though we have some sufferings, still we will be full of joy. Although we may have some hard times in our family and in the church, still we will be full of joy. The more we are willing to suffer, the more joy we will have; the more joy we have, the more we will be transformed. Eventually, a godly character will be manifested.

Hence, we are not speaking about character as the product of the so-called nurturing of human nature. Rather, we are speaking about the kind of character that God wants. After we have the Lord's life and Spirit in us, we begin to receive the breaking and the consuming, so that the Lord, in His life, can add more of Himself as the Spirit into us for our transformation, which issues in the character that God wants. In order to be useful in the service to the Lord, we need to receive a great deal of training in our character. The progress of character training altogether depends on the extent of transformation, and transformation is related to the growth in life, the knowledge of the truth, and the daily filling of the Holy Spirit. All these matters complement one another and require our earnest pursuit.

PURSUING THE KNOWLEDGE
OF GOD'S ETERNAL ECONOMY

Besides the four points mentioned above, we need to pursue so that we may see and know God's eternal economy. This is the deepest utterance in the Bible. The word *economy* may also be translated as *intention, plan, arrangement,* or *dispensation.* If we desire to be those who follow the Lord, it is not adequate merely to grow in life, pursue the truth, be filled with the Holy Spirit, and be transformed in our character. We also must know the economy of God.

Ephesians 3:11 says, "According to the eternal purpose which He made in Christ Jesus our Lord." The eternal purpose made by God is His economy. In Greek, the word for *eternal* means "of the ages," and the word for *purpose* means "plan." Hence, the eternal purpose of God and the economy of God are not two things; they are just one thing. The eternal purpose is the eternal plan that God made in eternity past, and this eternal plan is God's economy. The carrying out of God's economy is God's operation. Economy is an intrinsic plan, while operation is the practical carrying out of the economy.

The Greek word for *economy* is *oikonomia,* which means "household law," "household management," "household administration," and, derivatively, "a dispensation, a plan, for administration." The Bible shows us that God has an economy in Himself, and this economy includes God's eternal purpose, plan, dispensation, and intention. When this economy is revealed and carried out, it is His operation.

In order to know the economy of God, we must study Ephesians 1:9-11 and 3:9-11. We all need to study these six verses thoroughly and remember them by heart. These six verses are all concerning God's economy as the mystery of mysteries. If we recite and study them well, we will enjoy the benefit for our entire life.

CHAPTER TWO

CONCERNING THE ECONOMY OF GOD

Ephesians 1:10 says, "Unto the economy of the fullness of the times," and 3:9 says, "And to enlighten all that they may see what the economy of the mystery is, which throughout the ages has been hidden in God, who created all things." In Greek, the word for *economy* is not hard to comprehend, but its usage in the New Testament is not so easy to understand. This word is used in the New Testament with this meaning only by the apostle Paul. In Luke 16 when the Lord Jesus spoke about the unrighteous steward, He used this word, which in these verses is translated *stewardship* (vv. 2-4). A form of this word is also used in 1 Peter 4:10 where it is translated as *stewards*. However, in these two portions of the Scriptures this word does not bear much significance. Therefore, in the New Testament Paul is the only one who used this term from the viewpoint of God's New Testament economy. He used it three times—twice in Ephesians (1:10; 3:9) and once in 1 Timothy (1:4)—with direct reference to God's New Testament economy.

Although Paul referred to God's New Testament economy in 1 Timothy, it was still in relation to the church in Ephesus. In 1 Timothy 1:3-4, Paul said to Timothy, "I exhorted you...to remain in Ephesus in order that you might charge certain ones not to teach different things...rather than God's economy, which is in faith." Therefore, we can see that the three times Paul used this word in direct reference to God's New Testament economy were all concerning the church in Ephesus. He used it twice in Ephesians, speaking directly to the church in Ephesus, and once in 1 Timothy, speaking in relation to the church in Ephesus. In other words, God's speaking in the New Testament concerning His New Testament economy was altogether directed to the church in Ephesus. This is very meaningful.

THE DEFINITION OF THE WORD *ECONOMY*

The Greek word for *economy* is composed of two words. The first word *oikos* means "house" or "home," denoting a household or a dwelling place; the second word *nomos* means "law." When these two words are combined together, it means "household law," and it may be explained further to mean "household administration." Hence, the word *economy* means "household law," "household management," or "household administration." Since it is a household administration, it implies an arrangement or a plan. Since the household administration is to enforce the household rules, naturally it has an arrangement with a plan. Since it is an arrangement or a plan, there must also be a purpose.

The Usage of *Dispensation* ("Age" or "Arrangement") in Theology

When there is an arrangement or a plan, there is a purpose, and this arrangement or plan with a purpose constitutes a household administration. The arrangement of a household administration is mainly for distributing. What does it distribute? It distributes the riches of the family for the family's use. This word was used in relation to the big families in ancient times, which were similar to big Chinese households composed of a whole clan living together. When a big clan lives together, surely there are household laws and regulations, and surely there is the arrangement of the household administration. This arrangement is mainly to distribute the riches of the family for the living of the family members. This kind of distribution is a "dispensing." From the word disensing comes another word—*dispensation,* denoting the dispensation of economy. But when this word is used in theology to explain theological doctrines, it is usually understood as "age" or "period."

The Four Ages (Dispensations) in the Bible

Why is it that in theology the term *dispensation* is understood as "age"? It is because the dispensation of every period is actually the period itself. According to the record of the Bible, the dispensation of God's economy can be divided into four great periods. The first period is the dispensation of the patriarchs, the second period is the dispensation of law, the third period is the dispensation of grace, and the fourth period is the dispensation of righteousness executed in the kingdom. In other words, God's dispensation in the first period is concerning the patriarchs, and it can be called the dispensation of the patriarchs. This age, which was from Adam to Moses, lasted approximately two thousand five hundred years. God's dispensation in the second period is concerning His dealing with men by the law, and it can be called the dispensation of the law. This age, which was from the decree of the law by Moses to Christ's incarnation, lasted for about one thousand five hundred years. God's dispensation in the third period is concerning the application of the grace of Christ, and it can be called the dispensation of grace. This age, which is from the Lord Jesus' first coming to His second coming, should last for about two thousand years. God's dispensation in the fourth period is concerning God's execution of everything according to His righteousness, and it can be called the dispensation of righteousness. This will be the millennial kingdom, which will be from the Lord Jesus' second coming to the judgment at the great white throne, and will last for one thousand years.

In the old creation God has these four dispensations: the arrangement for the patriarchs, the administration by law, the supply by grace, and finally the execution according to righteousness. The patriarchs, the law, grace, and righteousness are God's four dispensations (arrangements). Consequently, these four dispensations (arrangements) spontaneously form four ages: the age of the patriarchs, the age of the law, the age of grace, and the age of the kingdom. First was the age of the patriarchs. After the age of the patriarchs was the age of the law. After the age of law is the age of grace. After the age of grace will be the age of righteousness, the age of the kingdom. These ages will last for a total of approximately seven thousand years.

The Bible Revealing the Years of Creation

It is difficult to calculate the number of years since the creation of the heavens and the earth. This is because before the creation of Adam there was another world, the preadamic world. According to the study of geologists, no one knows how many millions of years that world lasted. In fact, it is very hard to have an accurate calculation since the calculations by astronomers also vary. Hence, it is hard to say how many years the world before the creation of Adam lasted.

In the record of the entire book of Genesis, only verse 1 of chapter one refers to the preadamic world. This verse says, "In the beginning God created the heavens and the earth." No one knows how long ago this "beginning" was. Verse 2a goes on to say, "But the earth became waste and emptiness, and darkness was on the surface of the deep." This indicates that the world at that time was in chaos and had been terminated. No one knows how much time elapsed after the earth had been covered with darkness under deep water before God came in to do the work of re-creation, not creation. Verse 2b says, "And the Spirit of God was brooding upon the surface of the waters." At this time the Spirit of God was moving and brooding upon the surface of the waters to begin His work of re-creation. God firstly divided the light from the darkness, then He separated the waters which were under the expanse from the waters which were above the expanse (vv. 3-8). This was still not creation but only restoration. After this, God gathered together the waters under the heavens into one place to form the sea, and He let the dry land appear from underneath the water (vv. 9-10). This also was not creation but only a restoration. After the dry land had appeared, God caused the earth to grow plants. This, however, was not restoration but creation. Thus, God created the plants (vv. 11-13).

Then God began to restore the heavens and caused the sun, the moon, and the stars to appear (vv. 14-19). It is hard to say whether this was creation or restoration because verse 16 says, "And God made the two great light-bearers, the greater

light-bearer to rule the day and the lesser light-bearer to rule
the night." Moreover, God created the fish, that is, the living
creatures in the water. At the same time, He also created the
birds, that is, the living creatures in the air (vv. 20-23). Furthermore, He created the living creatures on the dry land,
which consisted mainly of three categories—cattle, beasts,
and creeping things (vv. 24-25). In this way living creatures
were generated in the seas, on the land, and in the air. These
records show that the re-creation which began from Genesis
1:2 includes both restoration and creation.

The most prominent thing in God's re-creation is that He
created man on the sixth day. Concerning the creation of
man, the Bible uses three different terms—*created, made,*
and *formed.* Verse 26 says, "And God said, Let Us make man
in Our image, according to Our likeness." Here the word *make*
is the same word used in the past tense in verses 7 and 16.
Verse 27 says, "And God created man in His own image." The
word *created* here is also used in verse 21. Verse 7 of chapter
two says, "Jehovah God formed man with the dust of the
ground." The word used here is *formed.* The Hebrew word for
created is *bara.* To create means to produce something out of
nothing. The Hebrew word for *made* is *asah.* To make means
to work upon an existing substance in order to produce something out of it. The Hebrew word for *formed* is *yatsar.* To form
means to give shape to something in the same way that a
potter molds clay into a form.

Man was not only created but also made and formed by
God. This is because God used the dust of the ground (2:7;
3:19), which already existed there, as material to make man a
physical body. Therefore, God used an existing substance to
make the final product—man's physical body, and He also
formed man in the same way that a potter molds a vessel. God
used the dust to form man's shape and then breathed into
him the breath of life. This breath of life, which came out from
God, became the spirit in man. Thus, man was enlivened and
became a living soul with a spirit. Hence, man was made and
formed by God. However, the spirit of man was created by God
because it came from the breath of life which came out of God.

Hence, God's original creation (1:1), particularly the creation of the heavens and the earth, was in the age long before Adam. We have no way to count the number of years of this age. However, if we count from Adam until the millennial kingdom, it should be a little over, if not exactly, seven thousand years.

The Seventy Weeks

Another set of years in the Bible that deserves our study is the seventy weeks in Daniel 9. These seventy weeks are divided into seven weeks, sixty-two weeks, and one week, which is the last week (vv. 24-27). The first part, composed of seven weeks, is forty-nine years, beginning with the issuing of the decree to rebuild the holy city by King Artaxerxes. In this period the rebuilding of the holy city Jerusalem, with street and trench, was completed (v. 25). Then the second part, composed of sixty-two weeks, is four hundred thirty-four years following the first seven weeks and ending with the crucifixion of the Lord Jesus—the year when the anointed One, Messiah, was cut off (v. 26a). This means that four hundred years after the first seven weeks, the Lord Jesus was born. Thirty-three and a half years later, after the Lord's human living and crucifixion, was exactly the very last year of the second part, the sixty-two weeks. The two parts added together (seven weeks plus sixty-two weeks) is a total of four hundred eighty-three years. This is very meaningful.

The third part, the last part of the seventy weeks, is the last week, the "one week" (v. 27). This one week is the last seven years of this age, which will be divided into two halves. At the beginning of this one week, the seventh Caesar of the restored Roman Empire (Rev. 17:10) will make a firm covenant with Israel. In the middle of the week, this ruler, who is the Antichrist, will break this covenant. This will be the beginning of the great tribulation (Matt. 24:21, 15; Dan. 7:25; 12:7; Rev. 12:6; 13:5) which will end with the Lord's second coming (Matt. 24:15-30; Dan. 9:27b). However, in between this last week and the preceding sixty-nine weeks a period of mystery is inserted. The Lord Jesus said that the day of His coming back was not made known even to Him as the One who was God become man. He said, "No one knows, not even...the Son, but the Father only" (Matt. 24:36). For this reason, whether this period of mysteries will be two thousand years or more than two thousand years, no one knows.

The Type and Fulfillment of
the Great Human Image in Daniel 2

Now we will go on to Daniel 2 to see the great human image seen by Nebuchadnezzar in his dream (vv. 1, 31-35). The head of the image was of fine gold, the breast and the arms were of silver, the abdomen and the thighs were of bronze, the legs were of iron, and the feet were partly of iron and partly of clay. Daniel said that the head of gold referred to Nebuchadnezzar (v. 38b). History proves that the Babylonian Empire with Nebuchadnezzar as king was indeed that head of gold. After the passing away of Babylon, a political situation emerged that was of two parts (7:5), typified by the silver breasts and arms. Its fulfillment in history was Medo-Persia—Medo (Media) being one nation, with Persia being another nation. These two nations shared equal power (cf. 5:31; 6:1) like the two shoulders of a person. After Medo-Persia ended, there were the abdomen and the thighs of bronze, signifying the Macedonian-Grecian Empire founded by Alexander. Daniel said that this kingdom would "rule over all the earth" (2:39). History tells us that Alexander won all the battles he fought. After crossing the Aegean Sea, he conquered Asia Minor and went on to attack the land of Palestine. At that time the Jews were a little indifferent toward him and did not supply him with provisions, so he was angry in his heart. However, as he was entering into Jerusalem after arriving in the land of Judea, the Jewish priests acted wisely. They all came out and lined up to welcome him and thus allayed his anger. They also led him to the temple and read to him the book of Daniel. Understanding the words in the book concerning himself, he was exceedingly happy and dealt with the Jews favorably.

However, history tells us that Alexander died at the early age of thirty-three and that his kingdom was divided into four sections, which were ruled by his four generals (11:3-4). Once the abdomen and the thighs ended, the Roman Empire, typified by the iron legs, came. Later the Roman Empire was divided into two parts, the eastern part and the western part, signified by the two iron legs. The Roman Empire lasted for a long time until a few years after A.D. 470, when the western Roman Empire was terminated and only the eastern Roman Empire remained. History points out that after the passing away of the Roman Empire, democracy began to gain ground in the European countries. Thus, the monarchs gradually became symbolic leaders, and the real authority was turned over to the people. This is signified by the feet of half-iron and half-clay, because clay symbolizes the people.

Daniel 2 also mentions four kinds of metals: gold, silver, bronze, and iron, representing four kinds of authority and glory. Gold is the most honorable one; silver is less honorable than gold; bronze is less honorable than silver, and iron has no honor but is solid and strong. This means that during the Babylonian age, the age of gold, the monarchs were not only dictatorial but also honored by the people. Later, the monarchs received less honor during the times of Medo-Persia and of Greece. Then, at the time of the Roman Empire they received even less honor because there was a senate with great authority. For example, Augustus did not install himself but was installed by the senate to be the Roman Caesar. This means that although the Roman Empire was very powerful, it did not have much honor; hence, it is iron. After the iron, what followed was something partly of iron and partly of clay. This means that what came out was partly democratic and partly dictatorial, or partly democratic and partly monarchic (constitutional monarchy). Up to this day, countries such as Great Britain, Norway, Denmark, the Netherlands, and Japan still maintain this kind of political system. They still have the establishment of the crown in some form. They are all half-iron and half-clay, having iron and clay mixed together. It is even more so in communist countries. They honor the people in word but in reality are totally dictatorial. Thus, they are also a mixture of iron and clay, being partly iron and partly clay.

For this reason, it is hard, even impossible, to count how long this period of partly iron and partly clay will last. But no matter what, the length of time covered by the feet and that covered by the legs are more or less the same. At this point in history, we should be at the upper part of the feet of the great human image. The great human image which Nebuchadnezzar saw begins with the head of gold, that is, the Babylonian Empire, and ends with the ten toes, that is, the ten nations that will be united to form the restored Roman Empire (Rev. 17:12-13). According to the prophecy of the Bible, and according to the history and situation of the world, although the Lord Jesus may not come back within the next few years, the time should not be too far away.

The Dispensation of the Age of Grace

Concerning these four ages, it is hard to ascertain the number of years of the third age, the age of grace. The reason is that the length of time between the sixty-two weeks and the last week is a mystery. The interval between the sixty-two weeks and the last week is the age of grace. This age lasts from the calves, which are below the knees, to the toes of the great human image. This period of time is difficult to calculate. Concerning the head, the breast and the arms, the abdomen and the thighs, and the two legs of the great human image, history has already demonstrated clearly that they refer to the four empires—Babylon, Medo-Persia, Macedonia-Greece, and Rome. In particular, the two legs refer to the Roman Empire. In the Bible iron signifies authority (Rev. 12:5) and denotes dictatorship or autocracy. After iron ended, clay has been rising gradually. Clay signifies democracy and the rights of the people, because man was created by God with the dust of the earth. For people to have rights is related to clay. Up to the present, the presidents of the United States have strongly advocated human rights. This means that they preferred to have a great amount of clay. However, the communist countries prefer to have a great amount of iron, so they are countries with "iron curtains." This is the mixture of partly iron and partly clay, yet the two "will not cleave to one another" (Dan. 2:43). Not only is it hard to calculate the years in this period, but this period itself is even a mystery.

The Four Dispensations in God's Economy

The four dispensations in God's eternal economy—the dispensation of the patriarchs, the dispensation of law, the dispensation of grace, and the dispensation of righteousness—in their practical carrying out are actually four periods. Hence, the word *dispensation* is really hard to understand according to its literal meaning, and it is even more difficult to understand when used in theology. Therefore, practically it is best to use the word *age*. Accordingly, the dispensation of the patriarchs is the age of the patriarchs, the dispensation of law is the age of law, the dispensation of grace is the age of grace, and the dispensation of righteousness is the age of righteousness, the age of the kingdom.

GOD'S ECONOMY BEING
GOD'S HOUSEHOLD ADMINISTRATION

From the preceding paragraphs we can understand that *oikonomia* is God's household administration. In brief, it is God's administration. Ephesians 1:10 says, "Unto the economy of the fullness of the times"; this means "unto the administration, the household administration of God, of the fullness of the ages." God's administration or household administration is an arrangement in God's house. From this we see that it is best to translate this word into *economy,* the anglicized form of the Greek word *oikonomia.*

The cultural history of the whole world can be said to have been recorded in the Bible, because everything was created, arranged, and ordained by God. For example, we can see from the feet that are "partly of iron and partly of clay" that a long time ago the Bible referred to democracy. This helps us to understand the meaning of the Chinese term *ching lun.* When we describe someone who is full of plans, intentions, and arrangements, we say that such a one is "filled with *ching lun.*" Regrettably, such an expression does not exist in the English language. Hence, in the English Recovery Version we use the word *economy.* Other English versions use *dispenation* instead of *economy.* For instance, the American Standard Version uses *dispensation* in Ephesians 1:10 and

3:9. Such a rendering does not clearly express the original meaning of the word and makes it hard for people to understand.

After a thorough study of human history, culture, and language with its usage, Webster's Dictionary was compiled. In this dictionary there are many definitions for the word *dispensation*. One of the definitions says that this word refers to "a divine ordering and administration of worldly affairs," and another definition says that it refers to "a period of history during which a particular divine revelation has predominated in the affairs of mankind." This means that there is an administration in every age or period, and the age itself can be referred to by the administration in that age. Therefore, in God's economy there are the dispensations, or arrangements, of the age of the patriarchs, the age of law, the age of grace, and the age of righteousness.

THE CONTENT OF GOD'S ECONOMY

We have already seen what God's economy is, and we have also seen the dispensations of God in His economy in four ages. Moreover, we understand that God's economy is God's household administration. Now we will go on to see the content of God's economy. Ephesians 1:9-11, Ephesians 3:9-11, and 1 Timothy 1:4 are all concerning God's economy. Not only do we need to be familiar with these verses and their contents so that we may fully know the truth contained in them, but we also need to be constituted with this truth by constantly pondering over and being exercised in these verses in order to be able to further explain and preach this truth to others.

God's Economy Beginning with Adam and Concluding with the New Jerusalem

A person who serves the Lord must have a vision. The vision of God's economy has a beginning, a process, and a conclusion. The vision of this economy began with Adam, passes through at least seven thousand years, and will conclude with the New Jerusalem, that is, with the coming of the new heavens and the new earth.

We must see that the New Jerusalem has its initial

coming and that it also has its consummate coming, its full coming. The initial coming of the New Jerusalem will be in the millennial kingdom for one thousand years on a small scale. At that time, not all the saved ones, but only the overcomers, including the overcomers both in the Old Testament and in the New Testament, will participate in it. The overcomers are a group of God's people who are perfected, completed, and matured. They are the only people who are qualified to participate in the New Jerusalem in its initial stage. Although the majority of the saints are God's chosen and saved ones, they have not allowed the grace of God to work in them thoroughly. Hence, most of them have not become mature. They are typified by the five foolish virgins (Matt. 25:1-13). Therefore, they will still have to buy oil. This means that they will still need to be matured.

God's Matured People
Constituting the New Jerusalem

At the Lord's coming back, all believers will pass through His judgment seat to receive judgment from Him (2 Cor. 5:10). The matured overcomers will enter the kingdom to constitute the New Jerusalem in its initial stage. Hence, the New Jerusalem is not a physical city but a constitution of the matured people of God. Being constituted is different from being organized. Our body is constituted, not organized. A wooden table, however, is organized. Anything organized is inorganic and lifeless, and it can be taken apart and then put back together again. Government organizations and wooden tables are examples of this. However, anything constituted is organic and is constituted with life. It cannot be taken apart and then put back together. Our body is an example of this. In like manner, the New Jerusalem is an entity constituted with the chosen and matured people of God who have reached the maturity in life. It is a constitution in life of God's matured people. Therefore, the New Jerusalem is not a physical city but an organic constitution.

The Coming of the New Jerusalem in Two Stages

The New Jerusalem is a particular, organic constitution.

Its scale is still quite small in the millennial kingdom because it will be constituted only with the overcomers. The saints, including those in the Old Testament, who died without being matured are typified by the five foolish virgins. That they all died is signified by the virgins becoming drowsy and falling asleep (Matt. 25:5). In the millennial kingdom God will cast them out into the outer darkness to be dealt with and disciplined (8:12; 22:13; 25:30). Therefore, in the present age, the age of grace, God supplies man with grace. However, in the age of the millennial kingdom God will deal with man according to righteousness. At that time there will be no more grace but only righteousness. God will deal with His people righteously. This dealing is to compel us to receive grace and be matured in this age.

All God's immature people, whether in the Old Testament or the New Testament, will be cast out into the outer darkness during the millennial kingdom so that they may be dealt with and become matured. After they have become matured, the new heaven and new earth will come, and they will be incorporated with the New Jerusalem of the millennial kingdom to be constituted into a great New Jerusalem. Thus, the coming of the New Jerusalem has two stages: the initial stage as a miniature and the completing stage as the consummation. The initial coming is in the millennial kingdom, and the complete and full coming is in the new heaven and new earth. This is the main content of God's economy.

THE WAY GOD CARRIES OUT HIS ECONOMY

What is the purpose of God in accomplishing His economy? What does He intend to do? In His economy God intends, arranges, and plans to dispense Himself into His chosen, created, called, redeemed, and regenerated people. Therefore, God firstly chose us before the foundation of the world and then created us in time. Afterward, He called us and then redeemed us. After He redeemed us, He dispensed Himself into us and regenerated us. Thus, we became those who were not only created by God but also born of Him. Once we have God in us, we become those who are born of Him. We have His life and nature and have become His children (John 1:12-13).

Hence, God's economy is God's intention, plan, and arrangement, which is also His purpose and His heart's pleasure and delight. God's heart's desire and purpose is nothing other than to dispense Himself into His chosen, created, called, redeemed, and regenerated people. Moreover, He will also sanctify, renew, transform, and conform them. Eventually, He will glorify His people, bringing them into His glory.

THE DIVINE DISPENSING OF
THE DIVINE TRINITY

How does God dispense Himself into us? In order to dispense Himself into us, God has to be triune. The Triune God dispenses Himself through His Divine Trinity—the Father, the Son, and the Spirit. Ephesians is a book on the divine dispensing. From chapter one Paul begins to speak about this dispensing: first is the Father's selection, then the Son's redemption, and then the Spirit's application. The Father is the source, and all the riches are in Him. The Son is the embodiment of the Father, and all that the Father is, has, and can do are embodied in the Son. Furthermore, the Son is realized as the Spirit. Hence, the Son comes as the Father, and the Spirit comes into us as the Son. In this way, when we have the Spirit, we also have the Son and the Father. The Divine Trinity—the Father, the Son, and the Spirit—is the means by which God dispenses Himself into us.

It is by the Divine Trinity that God is able to dispense Himself into all His chosen, created, called, redeemed, and regenerated people. Hence, if we want to understand God's economy, we must know the Divine Trinity for the divine dispensing. We cannot know the divine dispensing without knowing the Divine Trinity. Therefore, at the end of 2 Corinthians Paul drew a conclusion, saying, "The grace of the Lord Jesus Christ and the love of God and the fellowship of the Holy Spirit be with you all" (13:14). This is God dispensing Himself into us through His Divine Trinity.

The Divine Trinity carries out His divine dispensing through the divine Spirit. Today we all must be filled with this Spirit. When we are filled with this Spirit, we are filled with the Triune God. There is a good portrait of this in the Old Testament: the totality of three generations of men—Abraham, Issac, and Jacob. This is, in fact, the best illustration of this matter. In Exodus 3:15 God said, "Jehovah...the God of Abraham, the God of Isaac, and the God of Jacob....This is My name." This means that God is God the Father, God the Son, and God the Spirit. As God the Father, He is the source—He is the One who plans, chooses, decides, and arranges. As God the Son, He is the course—He is the One who accomplishes the Father's plan. Whatever we need, He has accomplished for us. We need to deal with sin, the world, the flesh, the corrupted self, Satan, and all our problems before God, yet He has already accomplished everything for us. God the Son went to the cross with seven statuses: the Lamb, a man in the flesh, the last Adam, the Firstborn of all creation, the bronze serpent, the Peacemaker, and a grain of wheat. In this way He accomplished an all-inclusive death and dealt with all our problems. Then, with the riches of all that He is and has, He has been realized as the Spirit and has come into us that we may partake of all the fullness of the Triune God.

The chorus of *Hymns*, #608 says, "The Triune God has now become our all!" This hymn clearly explains how the Triune God has become our blessed portion and how He is dispensing Himself into us. In Ephesians 3:8 the apostle Paul said, "To me...was this grace given to announce to the Gentiles the unsearchable riches of Christ as the gospel." Here *to announce* means not only "to preach" but also "to transmit." This means that Paul received a commission from God to transfuse the unsearchable riches of Christ into the Gentiles so that they all would have the Triune God in them. In this way they could become the members of Christ and, aggregately, the Body of Christ (v. 6). The revelation in Ephesians concerning the Body of Christ and the members of Christ is very complete and thorough.

The riches of the Lord are boundless. He is "without father, without mother, without genealogy; having neither beginning of days nor end of life" (Heb. 7:3). He is the unlimited and immeasurable One, and we can never exhaust our speaking of Him. Since He is such a rich God, His economy is also unsearchable. His desire is to dispense Himself into His chosen, created, called, redeemed, and regenerated people, and He is doing this through His Divine Trinity. The Divine Trinity is just God Himself. God Himself became the means through which this matter is accomplished. Today the Triune God has already been consummated as the life-giving Spirit to be dispensed into us (1 Cor. 15:45b). We must contact Him daily and exercise our spirit constantly to contact Him, commune with Him, and fellowship with Him as the Spirit. In this way all the divine riches of the Divine Trinity will be continually transfused into us to constitute us into the Body of Christ. In the millennial kingdom we will be constituted into the New Jerusalem in its initial stage, and eventually in the new heaven and new earth we will be constituted into the New Jerusalem in its consummate stage for eternity. This is the accomplishment of God's economy.

CHAPTER THREE

FOUR GREAT MATTERS IN THE BIBLE

Scripture Reading: Gen. 1:26-27; John 14:16-20; 16:13-15; Matt. 28:19; Eph. 2:18; 3:14-19; 4:4-6; 2 Cor. 13:14; Rev. 1:4-6.

The One into whom we believe is the divine and mysterious Triune God. Because it pleased the Triune God to reveal Himself to His children, He used the limited language of mankind to make known, in time, His heart's desire in the Bible. When we study the whole New Testament in depth, we can see that He revealed four great matters: first, the economy of God; second, the dispensing of God; third, the union of God with the believers; and fourth, the corporate expression of God.

FOUR GREAT MATTERS AND FOUR LAYERS OF VEILS

These four matters are so great, so high, and so mysterious that they are beyond human understanding. They have been revealed in a very special way in the Bible, in particular in the New Testament. Hence, readers of the Bible should ask the Lord for a spirit of wisdom and revelation lest they do not see the light of these four matters because of the influence of their natural, human, religious, and moral concepts. Everyone who reads the Bible has a fourfold problem—natural concepts, human concepts, religious concepts, and ethical concepts. The problem of these four kinds of concepts becomes a thick four-layered veil that covers our inner eyes. Unless we remove every one of these four layers of veils, it will be difficult for us to see the four divine matters revealed in the Bible.

JOHN THE BAPTIST LIVING IN A "WILD" WAY
AS THE FORERUNNER IN THE NEW TESTAMENT

Perhaps some will ask, "If we reject our moral, religious,

human, and natural concepts, won't we be abnormal?" This is exactly what we will be! At the beginning of the New Testament a forerunner appeared—John the Baptist. While he was still a child under the care of his parents, he could not decide anything on his own. However, when he began his ministry after he had become a full-grown man, he acted contrary to what is natural, contrary to what is human, contrary to religion, contrary to morality, and even contrary to culture. In his behavior we see that he was against these five categories of things.

The first thing that John the Baptist did was to leave everyone and go live alone in the wilderness. According to the statutes of the law, since he was born into a priestly family and his father was a priest, he was a priest by birth. According to the Old Testament regulations, a priest should have lived near the temple, and he should have spent most of his time serving in the temple (at least in the outer court if not within the sanctuary). However, John the Baptist not only did not stay in the holy temple, he did not even stay in the holy city, Jerusalem. Instead, he left the people to live alone in the wilderness. He did not just go to the wilderness to work during the day and then return to the holy city to rest at night. The Bible says that he lived in the wilderness (Luke 1:80). Furthermore, he wore a garment of camel's hair and a leather girdle, and ate locusts and wild honey. Everything in his living was "wild." This indicates that he had abandoned everything natural, everything human, and all the things of tradition, religion, ethics, and culture. This is the forerunner in the New Testament.

At the beginning of the New Testament dispensation this forerunner took the lead to stand against everything natural and everything of tradition, religion, ethics, and even culture. Regrettably, almost none of the Bible expositors, including theologians, have a clear idea about the significance of the living of John the Baptist. No one has ever pointed out that John lived in the *wild*erness and that he ate locusts and *wild* honey. The place where he stayed and the food that he ate were all *wild*. We may say that his food, clothing, dwelling, and transportation were all wild. He left the people to live alone, not in the holy temple, nor in the holy city, nor in his priestly home, but in the wilderness. He lived and worked in the wilderness; all his living and all his activities were carried out in the wilderness. Furthermore, the garment he wore was not woven by human labor; rather, it was a garment of camel's hair. There is no clear record in the Bible that shows how this garment of camel's hair was made. However, we can be sure that there was not much fine workmanship at that time. It is very likely that John simply put the camel's skin with the camel's hair upon himself as a garment. Moreover, he had "a leather girdle around his loins" (Matt. 3:4). Like the garment of camel's hair, this leather girdle was probably not made with much workmanship. A strong proof of the way John the Baptist lived is that his food was locusts and wild honey. In any case, after reading the record of John's living, people always have the impression that John had a *wild* flavor.

THE MINISTRY OF JOHN THE BAPTIST—
TELLING PEOPLE TO REPENT
FOR THE KINGDOM OF THE HEAVENS
WHICH WAS DRAWING NEAR

Why is it that the living of John the Baptist was so "wild"? The way a person lives should match the kind of occupation he has. For example, one who serves as a soldier should put on a military uniform, and one who serves as a doctor should wear a doctor's robe; otherwise, they will not be able to fight or work. Since John was born a priest, he should have worn the priestly garment and should have ministered in the temple. Why then did he choose to live in the wilderness, to clothe himself in a wild way, and to eat wild things? Moreover, when he went out to minister, the words of his preaching were also wild. In Matthew 3:1-2 we are told that he appeared, preaching in the wilderness of Judea, saying, "Repent, for the kingdom of the heavens has drawn near." According to grammar, this word was spoken altogether in the imperative mood. John did not tell people that they "should" or "ought to" repent; rather, he said, "Repent!" His tone was very direct, wild, and unrefined.

Furthermore, John baptized people in water after they had

repented. He did not use the word "bury," which is a more refined expression. When a person dies, he needs to be properly buried; this is human culture. John, however, "baptized" people in water instead of "burying" them (Matt. 3:11). *Baptized* in Greek has the meaning of "dipped." This kind of expression is quite "wild." When John saw many of the Pharisees and Sadducees coming to his baptism, he said to them, "Offspring of vipers, who prompted you to flee from the coming wrath?" (v. 7). He did not act at all like a refined preacher, for when he saw the religionists, he rebuked them, calling them "offspring of vipers." Would you not consider him as acting "wildly"?

He behaved in this way to show that he came with the intention to stand against culture, religion, naturalness, tradition, and morality. In the same principle, today when we read the Bible, we must also be against these five matters. This is by no means saying that we should be people who are immoral; instead, what we mean is that we need to take John the Baptist as our pattern. When the crowds asked him, saying, "What then shall we do?" John answered, "He who has two tunics, let him share with the one who has none; and he who has food, let him do likewise." At that time some tax collectors also came. They collected taxes for the Roman Empire from their fellow Jews, who were a weak and small people. When they asked John what they should do, John did not tell them to resign from being tax collectors, because he was not there to oppose imperialism. He just said, "Exact nothing more than what you have been ordered to." And when some serving in the military also asked him what they should do, he answered, "Extort nothing from anyone by force, nor take anything by false accusation, and be content with your wages" (Luke 3:10-14). From this we see that John was an ethical person. Nevertheless, he put ethics aside in his walk and living. This is because he knew that he did not come for morality and things of this nature but for preaching the kingdom of God.

For this reason, in the beginning of his ministry John preached the kingdom of God, saying, "Repent, for the kingdom of the heavens has drawn near" (Matt. 3:2). What he meant was that everyone had to be prepared because the kingdom of the heavens, the kingdom of God, was drawing near. What is "the kingdom of God"? We must understand that the kingdom of God is God Himself. The Chinese often use *world* instead of *kingdom* in such terms as "animal world" and "vegetable world." In fact, in both Greek and English, these things are called the "animal *kingdom*" and the "vegetable *kingdom*." In the animal world are animals, and in the vegetable world are vegetables. Likewise, in the human world, the human kingdom, are human beings. The human world ceases to exist when human beings are removed from it. In the same principle, the kingdom of God is God Himself, and it is God Himself who becomes everything as the content of the kingdom of God. If God leaves, the kingdom of God will have nothing left in it. Let us take the lions in the zoo as an example. The place where the lions are kept may be called "the lion world" or "the lion kingdom"; but if the lions were taken away, the lion kingdom would cease to exist.

ENTERING INTO THE KINGDOM OF GOD, NOT THROUGH TEACHING BUT THROUGH REGENERATION

If we desire to serve the Lord and walk on His way for our whole life, we must have a pure knowledge of the Word according to God's revelation. We must see that the drawing near of God's kingdom is the drawing near of God Himself. We must also see that man's becoming a part of God's world is man's entering into God's kingdom. As soon as man becomes a part of God's world, man has entered into the kingdom of God. Nicodemus was concerned mainly with morality when he came to see the Lord and said to Him, "Rabbi, we know that You have come from God as a teacher" (John 3:2). He thought that the Lord had come from God to teach ethics. But the Lord immediately interrupted him and said, "Truly, truly, I say to you, Unless one is born anew, he cannot see the kingdom of God" (v. 3). The Lord Jesus was patient and refined. He was not like us; we are always so rude. What He meant in actuality was: "Do not speak nonsense. Have you not seen what John the Baptist did? Truly, truly, I say to you, Unless a person is born anew, he can by no means enter into the kingdom of God, and he cannot even see it." Nicodemus was anxious when he heard this word, so he asked, "How can a man be born when he is old?" The Lord Jesus answered, "Unless one is born of water and the Spirit, he cannot enter into the kingdom of God" (vv. 4-5). What He meant was: "You have to remember what John the Baptist said and go into the water first, and then I will baptize you into the Holy Spirit. Unless you are born of water and the Spirit, you cannot have a share in God's world; that is, you cannot participate in God's kingdom."

In order for a dog or a cow to enter and participate in the human world, the human kingdom, it has to receive the human life by being born again. A dog or a cow can be in the human kingdom only by birth. I was born a man with man's life, so naturally I entered into the human world, the human kingdom. When I am in the human world, I am in the human kingdom. Today we all are descendants of Adam born in the human world; we entered the human kingdom by being born of our parents. If we want to obtain the citizenship of a certain country or join a certain club in society, we need to meet certain requirements or pay a fee. To be in the human kingdom, however, the only requirement is to be born. In fact, we had already entered into the human kingdom even while we were still in our mother's womb. This is why the Chinese count the age of a person from the time he is conceived in the mother's womb.

Today God desires that we would enter into God's world, God's kingdom. According to our natural understanding, we would say, "This is wonderful! Lord, please teach me how to enter into the kingdom of God." But His answer would be: "How can I teach you? Even if I would teach you until you became an old man, you would still be a man. It is impossible for Me to make you God by teaching you. You cannot become God unless you are born anew of Him." For example, teaching is absolutely necessary when you are trying to get a monkey to act like a human. However, regardless of how much the monkey has been taught and how much the monkey is able to mimic human behavior, the monkey is still a monkey. The monkey cannot become a human unless it is born again of man. Thirty years ago when I first came to Taiwan, I went to the zoo and watched a show in which a monkey ate a meal with a knife and fork. When the monkey came out onto the stage, the trainer would hit it with a whip, and the monkey would stand up right away, put on a small cap, and pick up a knife and a fork. Then when the trainer would hit the monkey again, the monkey would start eating the meal like a Westerner. That kind of performance is an attempt to teach a monkey to enter into the human kingdom. In my opinion, however, no amount of teaching can enable the monkey to enter into the human kingdom. The monkey had the monkey's life and did not want to enter into the human kingdom. In fact, it was quite a suffering for the monkey to try to be in the human kingdom. The monkey was forced to learn obediently because of the whip that was flying at him. But once the performance was over, the monkey immediately climbed down from the table, exposing its real condition. Today all religions, including Christianity, are just like trainers teaching monkeys to enter into the human kingdom. In the end, however, man's true nature is completely exposed. A monkey having only the monkey life can enter only into the monkey kingdom; a monkey cannot enter into the human kingdom through education. In order to enter into the human kingdom, a monkey has to possess the human life.

To Repent Being to Have a Change of Concept

When the Lord Jesus told Nicodemus, "Unless one is born anew, he cannot see the kingdom of God," He seemed to be saying, "Nicodemus, you are wrong. I did not come to be a teacher. You have already had Moses as your teacher. He was quite old and lived to be one hundred twenty years of age. You have already received a great amount of teaching from him. I did not come to be such a teacher. For such a long time Moses taught you how to conduct yourselves as humans, yet regardless of how much you Pharisees and Sadducees have tried, you do not look like humans; rather, you look like vipers. You have to give up! No matter how much you are taught, you cannot get into the kingdom of God. The only way to enter into the kingdom of God is to receive God as life and to gain God Himself. This is regeneration. Therefore, to repent is to have a change in your concept. You have to change your concepts about Moses, your concepts about the law, and even your worldly, natural concepts about serving God. All these concepts need to be changed. Therefore, you must repent!"

In our study of the Bible we need to pay attention to the background. John the Baptist came out and said, "Repent!" In actuality, this word may be translated as "have a change of concept," which means to have a change in our thinking and in our philosophy. In Greek, the basic definition of this word is to have a change of mind issuing in regret and thereby to have a turn in purpose; hence, the sense it conveys is stronger and more serious than the common understanding of the word *repent*. At that time the Jews, particularly the Pharisees, were filled in their mind with Moses' teachings and laws. They thought about and discussed Moses and the law all day long. This is why John told people to change their concept.

The changing of one's concept is a strict requirement. Unless this happens, no one can enter into the kingdom of God. The law of Moses taught people how to conduct themselves. It said, Do not murder, do not lie, do not steal, do not bear false testimony, honor your parents, and earnestly care for others. Moses' teachings, however, could only cause people to be lawful in the human kingdom; they could not bring them into the kingdom of God. It was in this situation, with this background, that John came. From the very beginning he told people to have a change of concept because God's world, God's kingdom (which is God Himself) had drawn near and was right at the door. Hence, John charged people to change their concept quickly, not to hold on to Moses any longer, and to have a turn in purpose by receiving Jesus Christ (who was God become man, who was the very God Himself, and who was the reality of the kingdom of God). This is to have a change of concept, a change from the law to God Himself and from Moses to Jesus Christ. Only by receiving Him can men enter into the kingdom of God.

To Enter into the Kingdom of God
Being to Receive God into Us

Now we all understand that the kingdom of God is God Himself. Following John the Baptist, the Lord Jesus also said, "The kingdom of God has drawn near" (Mark 1:15) when He went out to minister. In other words, John was saying, "God is on the way; He has drawn near." For example, if you have a friend who is coming to visit you, and he is already on the way, then you will say, "My friend has drawn near. He will be here in just a short while, so I have to prepare to receive him." Similarly, to proclaim that the kingdom of God has drawn near is to declare that God Himself has drawn near and that men should get ready to receive Him into them. The way to prepare is to put away the old, natural concepts and to hold on to the New Testament revelation, knowing that to enter into God's kingdom is to receive God Himself. This is the central thought of the preaching of John the Baptist as the forerunner in the New Testament dispensation.

Our Understanding concerning
the Kingdom of God Being Incomplete

In the past we had a considerable amount of knowledge concerning the kingdom of God, and although our understanding was not wrong, it was definitely incomplete. In our understanding God's kingdom was merely God's reigning. This kind of understanding was based upon human realization more than upon God's revelation. If the kingdom of God is merely God's reigning and the realm of God's reigning, then this means that it is God controlling man. For example, when you are going to steal, He would not let you; when you are going to lose your temper, He would not allow you; when you are furious and are going to speak some angry words, He would stop you; when you are going to do a bad thing or say a bad word, He would warn you first, and if you refuse to listen, then He would chastise you. This kind of understanding and realization about the kingdom of God is too narrow.

Suppose you have a monkey and you want to teach the monkey how to enter into the human kingdom. With this intention, you may take a whip in your hands and try to teach the monkey to act like a man by using its two front legs as two hands to eat food and do other things. When the monkey does not obey your instructions, then you may whip the monkey. I am afraid that this is our common understanding of God's reigning, that every day there is a "whip" regulating us from outside. In actuality, God's reigning is not an outward matter but a matter of life. If a monkey could be regenerated, born again, to become a man and have the human life, this life would automatically regulate the monkey from within to live like a man. In this way, the monkey would automatically and naturally enter into the human kingdom. If this happened, then to try to make the monkey to live and walk like a monkey again would be a suffering to the monkey. Therefore, it is altogether a matter of the innate ability of life, not a matter of outward teaching and regulation.

Every kind of life has its particular nature and ability. Take the banana tree as an example. You do not need to worry that a banana tree will grow round bananas. If you were to say to the banana tree, "Please make sure that you do not grow round bananas but that you grow long bananas," the banana tree, if it could speak, would answer, "Thank you for your concern! However, there is no need for you to exhort me, because the banana life in me has the nature and ability to automatically regulate me and cause me to grow bananas in the shape of bananas." In the same principle, you do not need to make demands of, or teach, the apple tree or the pear tree. They will spontaneously grow fruit in the shape of apples and pears respectively.

The Kingdom of God
Being God Himself, the Life of God

We must have a clear understanding of the kingdom of God. God's kingdom is God Himself, and God's kingdom has God as its content. Moreover, this content is Jesus Christ, who is God incarnated to be a man and who is God Himself as the reality of the kingdom of God. John 3:3 says, "Unless one is born anew, he cannot see the kingdom of God." God's kingdom is a divine realm, and man must have the life of God to enter into it. As we said before, life itself is a kingdom, a world, and a regulating element. Similarly, God's kingdom is God Himself, and God Himself is life, having the nature, ability, and shape of the divine life, which forms the realm of God's reigning.

GOD BEING TRIUNE

If we desire to know the Bible and God's economy, we must change our natural, human, religious, and moral concepts so that we may receive God's revelation. In order to know the four great matters in the Bible, we must understand and be acquainted with the Scripture verses listed at the beginning of this chapter. Similarly, if we want to understand that God is triune, we need to be familiar with Luke 15, which gives the best illustration of this matter. That chapter consists of three sections concerning a shepherd, a woman, and a father. The shepherd signifies Christ, the Son, coming to find us. The woman signifies the Holy Spirit thoroughly illuminating us within. And the father signifies God the Father receiving us, fallen men, back to His house. We may say that in the entire New Testament Luke 15 is the chapter which most clearly unveils the mystery of the Divine Trinity, with a particular emphasis on the love of the Triune God toward sinners.

Now we come to the first Scripture passage concerning the four great matters in the Bible. Genesis 1:26-27 begins, "And God said, Let Us make man in Our image, according to Our likeness." The word for *God* here in Hebrew is *Elohim*. This word is plural in number, usually indicating three or more. In Hebrew there is the singular number, the dual number, and the plural number, while in English there is the singular number and the plural number. *Elohim* is in the plural number, usually referring to three or more. A brother named Newberry, who was in the Brethren Assembly, put out the Newberry Bible in which he added marks and notes to the King James Version. In this version, three lines were drawn next to the word *God* to indicate that the word is plural in number, referring to the Triune God. Because God is triune, He can say "Us" and "Our" when He is speaking to Himself. It is true that

God is one, yet He can speak to Himself in one another because He is also three. There is only one God, but He has the aspect of being three—the Father, the Son, and the Spirit.

THE DIVINE TRINITY IN THE CREATION

Before the creation of man, the Triune God, whom we also call the Divine Trinity, held a council of the Divine Trinity. We may say that there was a conversation within the Godhead before God created man. God said, "Let Us make man in Our image, according to Our likeness." To whom was He speaking when He said, "Let Us"? Could it be that He was speaking to the heavens and the earth, since Adam was not yet created at that time? By studying the context and pondering over the situation at that time, we can readily discover that it was God speaking to Himself and fellowshipping with Himself. Thus, based upon this, some Bible readers concluded that there was a council of the Godhead. For this reason we must realize that in preparation for the creation of man, God first held a council of the Godhead within Himself, in which the three—the Father, the Son, and the Spirit—of the Divine Trinity were all present.

CREATING MAN IN HIS IMAGE

The council of the Divine Trinity was concerned directly with the four great matters in the Bible: the economy of God, the dispensing of God, the mingling of God with the believers, and the corporate expression of God. According to Genesis 1:26-27, God "mobilized" His Trinity for the creation of man. The Bible does not say that while the Father was creating, the Son was standing and watching, and the Spirit was not doing anything. It was not so! Even before the creation of man, the three of the Divine Trinity were all present, and the Triune God said to Himself, "Let Us make man in Our image, according to Our likeness." This is very meaningful.

We should not take things for granted when reading the Bible. When we come to Genesis 1:27, we should question and try to find out what "image" means. The truth of the Bible is rich and many-sided, so it is not easy to answer this question clearly. In brief, God's image refers to what God is inwardly.

What man is, is mostly in his mind, emotion, and will. These three parts are all inward. God created us according to what He is intrinsically.

God Creating Man according to His Attributes— Love, Light, Holiness, and Righteousness

The image of God includes not only His being but also His attributes, the characteristics of His nature. According to the entire Bible, the attributes of God include love, light, holiness, and righteousness. The characteristics of a lawmaker are revealed through the laws he makes. In other words, the kind of laws a person makes express the kind of person he is. If you ask a bank robber to make laws, he will surely legalize bank robbery because he considers it something that deserves sympathy and compassion. Likewise, the Ten Commandments were enacted by God according to His own attributes. According to our study of the Ten Commandments, we can summarize them in four words: love, light, holiness, and righteousness. These four items are God's attributes.

According to His attributes of love, light, holiness, and righteousness, God created man with a conscience of morality and a concept of morality. Man is not a beast, for within man there is patience, brightness, holiness, and righteousness. This is why the Chinese have the saying: "Justice is inherent in man's heart." This indicates that righteousness and justice are not acquired by learning; rather, they are inherent in man. For example, when you buy something and the cashier gives you back too much change, you may be very happy, but even without being told, you know that this is not right. This is the inherent sense of righteousness. There is not such a sense in cats, dogs, and monkeys. They steal food without knowing that it is improper. However, if you steal food, even if it is your favorite food, you know within that it is not right to steal. What is this? This is the function of the conscience, which was created for us by God according to His attributes.

The faculties of our mind, emotion, and will, which constitute what we are, were created according to God's intrinsic being. Moreover, human beings delight in love, light, holiness, and righteousness because we were created in this way according to God's attributes. When God's attributes are expressed through us, they become our human virtues. Therefore, when the Chinese sages discussed the conscience, eventually they spoke about the "bright virtue," indicating that within man there is something bright and good. This is the conscience. Hence, we can say that God created man according to His love, light, holiness, and righteousness.

The Image of God Being His Beloved Son—Christ

Let us now consider several verses from the New Testament. Second Corinthians 4:4 says, "Christ, who is the image of God." Philippians 2:6 says, "[Christ] existing in the form of God." Colossians 1:15 says that Christ, the Son of God's love, "is the image of the invisible God." And Hebrews 1:3 tells us that Christ is "the impress of His [God's] substance." All these verses clearly show us that Christ is the image of God. Therefore, for man to be created in the image of God means that man was created according to Christ. In other words, what the created man is inwardly is altogether created according to Christ. The principle for the proper exposition of the Bible is to interpret the Bible both according to biblical facts and according to the biblical text itself. According to the fact, God created man in His image; that is, He created man according to His mind, emotion, and will and also according to love, light, holiness, and righteousness. According to the biblical text, the New Testament says that Christ, God's beloved Son, is the image of God. Hence, God also created man according to Christ. God created us in this way, expecting that one day we would receive and contain Christ.

Man Being Created
according to the Image of Christ
for the Purpose of Containing Christ

The way that man would be created was determined through the council of the Divine Trinity—the Father, the Son, and the Spirit. God said, "Let Us make man in Our image, according to Our likeness." The image here is neither the Father nor the Spirit but the Son. God created man in the image of the Son. In this respect, we are containers of Christ;

we were created to contain Christ. If Christ is "square" and we are "round," we will never be able to contain Him. Thus, God had to make us "square" just like Christ. Before we were saved, and even at birth, we were already created in the image of Christ to be exactly the same as Christ, so that we would be fit to receive Him. For this reason, once we received Christ and were saved, we felt so comfortable and at ease within. Let me use an illustration. When you purchase something, the salesperson often puts it in a box. The box that the salesperson uses is just right, being neither too large nor too small. This is not a coincidence, because the box was made precisely according to the shape of that particular item. Everyone who has received Christ has experienced this indescribable sense of comfort, because we were created in His image, and we were created for Him.

How then does Christ come into us? According to the New Testament revelation, the Son comes into us as the Spirit (John 14:17; 1 Cor. 6:17; 15:45; 2 Cor. 3:17; 2 Tim. 4:22). Without being the Spirit, the Son could not come into us. These truths are implied in Genesis 1:26-27.

SPENDING TIME TO STUDY THE TRUTH

Now we come to the second portion of the Word that we will discuss—John 14:16-20. These five crucial verses clearly unveil the Divine Trinity—the Father, the Son, and the Spirit. In verses 16-17 the Lord said, "And I will ask the Father, and He will give you another Comforter,...the Spirit of reality." These two verses show us the Divine Trinity—the Father, the Son, and the Spirit. The Lord said that the Spirit would come and enter into us.

The third portion from the Word is John 16:13-15. These three verses reveal to us the transmission of the Divine Trinity. All that the Father has is in the Son, all that the Son has is given to the Spirit, and all that the Spirit has is realized in us. In these verses the Lord said, "When He, the Spirit of reality, comes, He will guide you into all the reality; for He will not speak from Himself, but what He hears He will speak; and He will declare to you the things that are coming. He will glorify Me, for He will receive of Mine and will declare it to you. All that the Father has is Mine; for this reason I have said that He receives of Mine and will declare it to you." The work of the Holy Spirit is, first, to convict the world; second, as the Spirit of reality, it is to guide the believers into all the reality, to make all that the Son is and has real to the believers. All that the Father is and has is embodied in the Son (Col. 2:9), and all that the Son is and has is declared as reality to the believers through the Spirit (John 16:13-15). This declaring is the glorifying of the Son with the Father. Hence, it is a matter of the Triune God being wrought into and mingled with the believers.

The fourth portion is Matthew 28:19: "Baptizing them into the name of the Father and of the Son and of the Holy Spirit." This also implies the Divine Trinity. In this verse the Father, the Son, and the Spirit are three, yet the "name" is singular in number. This shows us that we have all been baptized into the unique name of the Father, the Son, and the Holy Spirit. The name is the sum total of the Divine Being, equivalent to His person. To baptize someone into the name of the Triune God is to immerse him into all that the Triune God is.

The fifth portion is Ephesians 2:18: "For through Him we both have access in one Spirit unto the Father." Both the Jewish and the Gentile believers have access to the Father through Christ, who abolished the law of the commandments in ordinances, broke down the middle wall of partition, slew the enmity to reconcile the Gentiles to the Jews, and shed His blood to redeem the Jews and the Gentiles to God. Here the trinity of the Godhead is implied. Through God the Son, who is the Accomplisher, the means, and in God the Spirit, who is the Executor, the application, we have access unto the Father, who is the Originator, the source of our enjoyment.

The sixth portion is Ephesians 3:14-19, which says that the Father will grant us to be strengthened with power through His Spirit into the inner man, that Christ, the Son, may make His home in our hearts through faith, with the result that we will be filled with the Triune God unto all the fullness of God.

The seventh portion is 2 Corinthians 13:14: "The grace of the Lord Jesus Christ and the love of God and the fellowship of the Holy Spirit be with you all." The grace of the Lord is the Lord Himself as life to us for our enjoyment, the love of God is God Himself as the source of the grace of the Lord, and the fellowship of the Holy Spirit is the Holy Spirit Himself as the transmission of the grace of the Lord with the love of God for our participation. These are not three separate matters but three aspects of one thing, just as the Lord, God, and the Holy Spirit are not three separate Gods but three "hypostases...of the one same undivided and indivisible" God (Philip Schaff). The Father, the Son, and the Spirit are the hypostases, the supporting substances, which constitute this one God.

The eighth portion is Revelation 1:4-6: "Grace to you and peace from Him who is and who was and who is coming, and from the seven Spirits who are before His throne, and from Jesus Christ, the faithful Witness, the Firstborn of the dead, and the Ruler of the kings of the earth. To Him who loves us and has released us from our sins by His blood and made us a kingdom, priests to His God and Father." He who is and who was and who is coming is God the eternal Father. The seven Spirits who are before God's throne are the operating Spirit of God, God the Spirit. Jesus Christ—"the faithful Witness" to God, "the Firstborn of the dead" to the church, and "the Ruler of the kings of the earth" to the world—is God the Son. This is the Triune God. From such a Triune God, grace and peace are imparted to the churches. At the opening of the other Epistles, only the Father and the Son are mentioned, and from Them grace and peace are given to the receivers. Here, however, the Spirit is included, and from Him grace and peace are imparted to the churches. Through the work of the Divine Trinity, we are made not only a kingdom to God but also priests to God (1 Pet. 2:5). The kingdom is for God's dominion, whereas priests are for the expression of God's image. This is the kingly, royal priesthood (v. 9), which is for the fulfillment of God's original purpose in creating man (Gen. 1:26-28).

These are the four great matters in the Bible: the economy of God, the dispensing of God, the union of God with us, and God's corporate expression in us.

CHAPTER FOUR

THE TRUTH OF THE MYSTERY IN THE GOSPEL OF JOHN

(1)

A BIRD'S-EYE VIEW OF THE GOSPEL OF JOHN

Of all the outlines in the New Testament Recovery Version, the outline of the Gospel of John may be considered the best. If we want to know a certain book thoroughly, we must begin with its outline. The outline of a book helps us to have a complete bird's-eye view of that book

Two Main Sections of the Gospel of John

From the outline of the Gospel of John we see that the entire book can be divided into two main sections. The first main section, chapters one through thirteen, concerns "The eternal Word incarnated coming to bring God into man." The second main section, chapters fourteen through twenty-one, concerns "Jesus crucified and Christ resurrected going to prepare the way to bring man into God, and as the Spirit coming to abide and live in the believers for the building of God's habitation." The crucified One is Jesus, while the resurrected One is Christ. Through Jesus' crucifixion and Christ's resurrection the way has been prepared for man to be brought into God. In brief, the first section of the Gospel of John speaks about bringing God into man, and the second section speaks about bringing man into God. How could God be brought into man? God was brought into man through the eternal Word's coming in His incarnation. How could man be brought into God? Man was brought into God through Jesus Christ's going in His death and resurrection. Therefore, His coming was accomplished in His incarnation, and His going was accomplished in His death and resurrection.

Moreover, after His resurrection He comes to us again as the Spirit. He came the first time in His incarnation. Then He went in His death and resurrection, and following this He comes again as the Spirit. He came in incarnation to bring God into man, and He went in death and resurrection to bring man into God. However, He was not able to accomplish His purpose just by His coming and His going. Thus, as the Spirit He comes again to abide and live in the believers for the building of God's habitation.

God's work is not done until His habitation is built up. Although God was brought into man, and man was brought into God, God still needs a habitation. In order to produce such a habitation, it is necessary that the Spirit come to abide and live in the believers. This is the bird's-eye view of the whole book of the Gospel of John.

The two main sections of the Gospel of John are as distinct as a person's eyebrows. Within the two main sections there are sub-points, and each sub-point has many small items that give further explanation. For example, the first main section, composed of thirteen chapters, is on "The eternal Word incarnated coming to bring God into man." The first sub-point, which is in chapter one, is: "Introduction to life and building." The first small item is: "The Word in eternity past, who was God, through creation coming as life and light to bring forth the children of God." This is covered in verses 1 to 13, concerning the eternal Word, who was God (v. 1), in whom was life, which was the light of men (v. 4), and in whom also were all things, for all things came into being through Him (v. 3). Therefore, life, light, and creation are included in this small item. The One who came in incarnation was such a One.

The Main Points of the Gospel of John

The first main section of the Gospel of John is divided into five sub-sections: first, "Introduction to life and building" (ch. 1); second, "Life's principle and life's purpose" (2:1-22); third, "Life meeting the need of man's every case" (2:23—11:57);

fourth, "Life's issue and multiplication" (ch. 12); and fifth, "Life's washing in love to maintain fellowship" (ch. 13).

The second main section, consisting of eight chapters, is "Jesus crucified and Christ resurrected going to prepare the way to bring man into God, and as the Spirit coming to abide and live in the believers for the building of God's habitation." This main section is divided into four sub-sections: first, "Life's indwelling—for the building of God's habitation" (14:1—16:33); second, "Life's prayer" (ch. 17); third, "Life's process through death and resurrection for multiplication" (18:1—20:13, 17); and fourth, "Life in resurrection" (20:14—21:25).

The sub-points in the outline are concise explanations, while the small items are detailed descriptions. For example, the third sub-section of the second main section is "Life's process through death and resurrection for multiplication," which is covered in 18:1—20:13, 17. These two and a half chapters, in brief, are concerning the Lord's death and resurrection. They can also be divided up in a detailed way into the following points: first, He was betrayed; second, He was arrested; third, He was judged; fourth, He was crucified; fifth, He was buried; and sixth, He was resurrected. This is the process that He went through—from His betrayal to His resurrection. He passed through this process for multiplication.

THE MYSTERY OF THE DIVINE TRINITY IN JOHN 14

In these three chapters—John 14, 15, and 16—the most important portion is 14:7-20. Before we present the main points of this section, however, we must firstly have a general knowledge about its position in the book. Chapter fourteen is included under the first sub-section of the second main section. In addition, this sub-section is further divided into three small sections. The first small section, which comprises all of chapter fourteen, is on "The dispensing of the Triune God—for the producing of His abode." This small section is further divided into four small points. The second point is "The Triune God dispensing Himself into the believers," and comprises verses 7 though 20. This is the point that we will cover. This small point is divided into two smaller points: first, "The Father embodied in the Son seen among the believers"

(vv. 7-14); and second, "The Son realized as the Spirit to abide in the believers" (vv. 15-20).

In 14:7 the Lord told the disciples, "If you had known Me, you would have known My Father also; and henceforth you know Him and have seen Him." After hearing this word, Philip said, "Lord, show us the Father and it is sufficient for us" (v. 8). Philip was somewhat puzzled by the Lord's speaking. Although he probably thought it was quite meaningful when he first heard it, he did not understand its real meaning; so he responded wrongly, asking the Lord to show them the Father. What the Lord meant when He said this to the disciples was that the disciples had seen the Father since they had already seen the Son. Philip, however, felt that although they had been seeing the Lord for such a long time, they had not yet seen the Father. They heard the Lord telling them to see, but in fact, they did not see anything. Therefore, out of ignorance he said that if the Lord would show them the Father, they would be satisfied.

Philip is actually a picture of us, and each one of us is a Philip. Not only the brothers are Philips, but the sisters are also Philips. Whoever speaks nonsensical words, words without any revelation, is a Philip. Today nearly all of Christianity is a Philip: the Catholic Church is a Philip, and the Protestant churches are also Philips. The so-called fundamentalists are Philips, the Pentecostalists are Philips, and, even more, the modernists are Philips (even evil Philips). Whoever preaches the word without knowing the mystery of the Divine Trinity is speaking nonsense and is therefore a Philip. Today nearly all of the preaching by Christianity is totally off-track and is far away from the central subject—the Divine Trinity. Anyone who does not base his speaking upon the revelation of the Divine Trinity speaks nonsense and is a Philip. Even when we are preaching the truth concerning justification by faith or concerning redemption through the precious blood, we must not preach these truths apart from the mystery of the Divine Trinity.

Bible teachers all know that the New Testament contains the four Gospels, which speak about four aspects of the Lord Jesus. This is so that an accurate picture will be presented.

Similarly, if you want to make a bronze statue of someone, you have to take four pictures of him so that you can have the basis to create the statue accurately, or else it may not look so real. At the beginning of the New Testament are the four Gospels: Matthew, Mark, Luke, and John. Most people agree that Matthew is on the Lord Jesus being the King, Mark is on the Lord Jesus being a slave, and Luke is on the Lord Jesus being a man. Concerning John, however, not many people have the boldness to say that it is on the Lord Jesus being God. If we do not have adequate revelation and knowledge concerning the mystery of the Divine Trinity unveiled in the Gospel of John, we surely will not have the boldness and confidence to say this. We need particular knowledge concerning the mysterious Triune God.

Let me use language as an example. In Chinese, some words are very close in pronunciation, and such words must be pronounced very carefully to avoid being misunderstood. I have been speaking Shantung Mandarin since my youth, so my pronunciation of standard Mandarin is usually not so precise. For example, my last name is "Lee," and Sister Lee's maiden name is "Li." When I say these two words, others often cannot make a clear distinction between "Lee" and "Li" because the pronunciation of these two words is so similar. Because of this, whenever someone asks me, "What is your wife's maiden name?" I always hesitate and do not have the boldness to say it because I am not sure if I will pronounce it correctly. In the same way, if we do not have a deep and thorough understanding of the words of mystery in the Gospel of John concerning the Triune God, we surely will not have the boldness to speak them.

In actuality, the mystery in the four Gospels is the same as the mystery in the Gospel of John, and the mystery in John is the Triune God.

The Word Being in the Beginning, and the Word Being God

With respect to the Lord's relationship to us, the first aspect of the mystery in the Gospel of John, as shown in the outline, is that the Lord Jesus is the Word. When the Lord came, He began to have a relationship with us as the Word. John does not begin with, "In the beginning was God," but he begins with, "In the beginning was the Word." The fact that God is referred to as the Word indicates that He has a relationship with man. Suppose I came to you and just looked at you, and let you look at me. If we just look at one another without saying anything, nothing will happen. Once I open my mouth to speak, however, a relationship begins. When I speak, you respond. When I speak again, you respond again. With such speaking and responding, a relationship develops. Such a relationship is initiated and formed by words. What is this? This is the story of the word. Words are the medium by which two parties develop a relationship. Every day news happens all over the world. We develop a relationship with the news because it is communicated to us through the words of the media, including radio, television, magazines, and newspapers.

In order to have a relationship with man, the Triune God must be the Word. If He were not the Word, He would have no way to have a relationship with the created man. Therefore, throughout the whole Bible the Word is very crucial. Even when God created all things, He did it through His word, which is Himself. For example, I am speaking to you now, and the words I speak are just myself. If I speak wrongly, not only my words will be condemned, but I myself will also be condemned. I am one with my words. The two—my words and I—are inseparable. If you were indicted in court for speaking wrongly and declared guilty by the judge, you could not say, "Your Honor, I am not wrong; it was my words that were wrong. You may condemn my words, but do not condemn me." John 1:1 says, "In the beginning was the Word, and the Word was with God, and the Word was God." The Word is God Himself.

FOUR STEPS TAKEN BY THE WORD
IN HIS RELATIONSHIP WITH MAN

In the beginning of the Gospel of John, John speaks about the Word. This proves that God wants to have a relationship with man. How can God have a relationship with man? The first step is that He was incarnated to bring God into man; the second step is that He lived a human life on earth for thirty-three and a half years; the third step is that through His death and resurrection He brought man into God; and the fourth step is that He became the Spirit to abide and live in those who have believed into Him.

Concerning Christ as the Spirit

The Last Adam Becoming the Life-giving Spirit

Concerning the fundamental truth of Christ being the Spirit, there are two crucial verses. The first verse is 1 Corinthians 15:45b, which says, "The last Adam became a life-giving Spirit." Some people argue that the life-giving Spirit here is not the Holy Spirit but the Spirit of Christ as a person. They say that just as we humans have a spirit, so Christ also has a spirit. They also say that when this Jesus Christ died, He became life-giving Spirit; however, this verse does not say that the last Adam simply became "Spirit," without any modifier. Rather, it says that He became "a life-giving Spirit," with the modifier "life-giving." This indicates that this Spirit can give life. May I ask, What kind of spirit can give life? Can the human spirit give life? If Jesus Christ had not become the Spirit, and if the Spirit in 1 Corinthians 15:45b refers only to the spirit He had as a man, can that human spirit give life? Since 1 Corinthians 15:45b says explicitly that He became a "life-giving" Spirit, then it simply means that He became a life-giving Spirit. That the last Adam became a life-giving Spirit is a very crucial revelation, and we cannot delete the word *life-giving* as it pleases us. Moreover, 2 Corinthians 3:6 says, "But the Spirit gives life." Only God can give life and enliven man. Besides God, no one in this universe can give life and enliven man.

The Lord Being the Spirit

The second crucial verse concerning Christ being the Spirit is 2 Corinthians 3:17, which says, "The Lord is the Spirit." "The Lord" here, of course, is Jesus, and "the Spirit" is the Spirit who gives life, mentioned in verse 6, and who is the life-giving

Spirit. Many Christian writers, including Dean Alford and Andrew Murray, all acknowledged this point. Praise the Lord, the Christ in whom we believe is the Spirit today.

The Lack in Christianity's Theology

In our English hymnal there are twenty to thirty hymns concerning Christ as the Spirit. In the compilation of the hymnal, we did our best to collect all the truths expressed in hymns from different Christian backgrounds. Therefore, our hymnal may be considered a collection of the hymns of theology. If you want to study real theology, you need to first study our hymnal.

A great lack in Christian theology is that it does not say anything about Christ being the Spirit. Due to the fact that this truth is lacking, it is impossible to link all other truths together. Without this truth, the Father is the Father, the Son is the Son, the Spirit is the Spirit and the three are totally separated. In other words, without Christ being the Spirit, the three of the Divine Trinity would be completely separated. From this standpoint, we must consider it our responsibility to explain and preach the divine truth concerning Christ being the Spirit according to the revelation of the Bible.

In particular, the young people who desire to serve the Lord must know this truth thoroughly. You should not be the Philips who speak nonsense. Rather, you should spend time to study in order that you would see this mystery in the Gospel of John, so that whatever you preach will involve this truth.

HE WHO HAS SEEN THE SON
HAVING SEEN THE FATHER

In John 14 Philip asked the Lord to show them the Father, and the Lord answered, "Have I been so long a time with you, and you have not known Me, Philip?" (v. 9a). After hearing this, Philip was even more puzzled. Perhaps he thought, "Of course, I know You. How could I not know You? You grew up in Nazareth, and You were a carpenter before You came out to preach the word. Your mother is Mary, whose husband is Joseph. You also have a few siblings, all of whom I know." In fact, if this was Philip's thought concerning what it meant to know Jesus, then this shows that he did not know Jesus at all. So the Lord went on to say, "He who has seen Me has seen the Father; how is it that you say, Show us the Father?" (v. 9b). Some Bible expositors think that this means that the Lord is the Father's representative. They would liken this to the President of the United States sending a representative to the Philippines: when the people there contact this representative, it is equivalent to contacting the President of the United States. Actually, this verse does not mean that the Lord Jesus represents God or that the Son of God represents the heavenly Father. What it means is that the Lord Jesus, the Son, is the Father. He does not merely *represent*, but He *is*.

When the Lord said, "How is it that you say, Show us the Father?", He meant that He is the Father; thus, when men see Him, they see the Father. The disciples' asking the Lord to show them the Father is like having the President of the United States come to see you and saying to him, "Please show us the President of the United States." He would surely be very surprised and say, "You who have seen me have seen the President of the United States; how is it that you say, 'Show us the President of the United States?'" The Lord had been with the disciples for three and a half years, and they had been seeing Him all that time, yet incredibly they still did not know that He was the Father and still asked Him to show them the Father. They were really making matters difficult for the Lord.

THE SON BEING IN THE FATHER
AND THE FATHER BEING IN THE SON

In verse 10 the Lord continued, "Do you not believe that I am in the Father and the Father is in Me?" Over the past eighteen hundred years this truth has been gradually neglected. However, the theologians in the early centuries considered this matter to be quite important. They even coined the theological term *coinherence,* meaning that you are in me, and I am in you, and we are in one another mutually. In Christianity's theology today, many teach the doctrine of the Trinity, and some advocate the use of the term *coexistence,* but not many have the boldness to use the term *coinherence*. Nonetheless, in early Christian theology both *coexistence* and *coinherence* were used. This is a tremendously great matter: the Son is in the Father, the Father is in the Son, and the Son and the Father are one. This is why the Lord asked Philip how it could be that he had seen the Son yet had not seen the Father.

THE SON SPEAKING
WHILE THE FATHER WAS WORKING

Furthermore, the Lord said, "The words that I say to you I do not speak from Myself, but the Father who abides in Me does His works" (v. 10b). This simply means that the Son speaks while the Father works. Perhaps some will say, "Is this not the same as what the Chinese refer to as playing *shuang-huang*.* *Shuang-huang* involves two persons, whereas here there is only one person: this One is He yet "I." "I" speaks while He works. The Son speaks, which is to express something outwardly. However, the Son does not speak according to Himself, but the Father who abides in the Son does His works. This indicates that the Son speaks outwardly while the Father works inwardly. The One who is outside speaks, while the One who is inside works. Therefore, are They two persons? We can say that They are two yet one, one yet two. Moreover, it is not that there is one who speaks without and another who works within. The One who works within is in the One who speaks without; that is, the Father is in the Son. At the same time, the One who speaks without is in the One who works within; that is, the Son is in the Father. Hence, the two are actually one. Their coinherence is an unfathomable mystery.

THE FATHER AND THE SON COINHERING
FOR THE DIVINE DISPENSING

Ultimately, we all have to admit that we really do not know all that we think we know. However, there is truly such a fact that the Son is in the Father, the Father is in the Son, and the two are one. This has been clearly shown in

---

* *Shuang-huang* is a Chinese variety act featuring two performers, one of whom speaks while the other acts out the gestures—Trans.

the Bible in black and white. Though They are one, there is still the aspect of Their being two; furthermore, though there is the aspect of Their being two, They are one. This is the mystery of the Divine Trinity.

What is the reason for the coinhering of the Father and the Son? It is for the divine dispensing. If God were not triune, if the Son did not speak outwardly while the Father worked inwardly there would be no possibility for God to dispense Himself into us. Moreover, God's dispensing is altogether a story of the "Word." For example, my speaking to you is a kind of dispensing. I am full of knowledge within; what should I do if I want to infuse you with all my knowledge? If I went and found a doctor, he would have no way to inject my knowledge into you. The most simple and effective way is for me to speak to you directly. The more I speak, the more I transmit all the knowledge within me into you. Hence, speaking is a dispensing. In the same way, when you work for the Lord, you need to learn to speak for the Lord so that you can dispense Him into others.

In ancient times when people engaged in war, they relied mainly on the weapons in their hands. Therefore, the Chinese say that a soldier who is skillful with his weapon can defend a key position single-handedly and that even ten thousand men cannot match him. If a soldier is not skillful with his weapon, he cannot fight the battle. If we want to fight the battle, we must have a weapon in our hands. Our "weapon" is the word, and we all should be experts at using this weapon. As experts, we should be able to strike more than just the air. Hence, we all need to be trained. What kind of training do we need? We need the training of infusing: we need to be infused with God's economy, and the more we are infused the better. Then one day we all will be able to do the same work of infusing God's economy into others. This is dispensing. John 14, 15, and 16 are all on the divine dispensing of the Divine Trinity, and this dispensing depends on speaking.

THOSE WHO BELIEVE INTO THE SON
DOING GREATER WORKS—
DISPENSING CHRIST THROUGH SPEAKING

In John 14:11-12 the Lord says, "Believe Me that I am in

the Father and the Father is in Me; but if not, believe because of the works themselves. Truly, truly, I say to you, He who believes into Me, the works which I do he shall do also; and greater than these he shall do because I am going to the Father." From the context of these verses we understand that doing greater works does not refer to doing greater miracles but to speaking, because previously the Lord said that the Son is speaking while the Father who abides in the Son is working. Similarly, our doing "greater works" refers to our speaking through which the Lord who abides in us does His work. Whenever we speak for the Lord, the Lord works in us. This is not for the purpose of performing a greater miracle but for dispensing. From both the book of Acts and church history we see that after the Lord's departure the apostles, such as Peter and Paul, did greater things than what the Lord did in the three and a half years when He was on the earth. On the day of Pentecost, Peter, who before this time spoke nonsensically, stood up and spoke a long message, and three thousand people were saved. What does it mean to be saved? It means to be infused and filled up with the word. Peter's message caused three thousand people to be infused. This is what the Lord meant when He said, "Greater than these he shall do."

After reading John 14 some may ask, "The Lord said clearly that we shall do greater works than He did. However, He raised people from the dead, but we cannot raise even a dead dog. He healed the sick and cast out demons many, many times, but we cannot do such things even once. What is the matter?" In order to understand the real significance of the Bible, we cannot interpret things out of context; we have to read everything in its context. According to the context of John 14:11-12, "greater" does not refer to greater signs or wonders but to the speaking which is for dispensing. While you are serving as a mouthpiece to release the Lord's speaking, He is in you doing His work. This is transmission, dispensing.

The Gospel of John shows us the Word from its outset: "In the beginning was the Word, and the Word was with God." After becoming flesh the Word began to speak, and today He continues speaking. While He speaks, the Father is being dispensed. Today in our work for the Lord, we also dispense Him through our speaking. This is the divine dispensing of the Divine Trinity as revealed in the Gospel of John.

We should not merely know the Bible on the surface, but we should go deeper to know the mysterious truth in the Bible. Only this truth can constitute us into another kind of person, enabling us to speak for God and to dispense God into others. This is the real purpose of our knowing the truth of the mystery in the Gospel of John.

CHAPTER FIVE

THE TRUTH OF THE MYSTERY
IN THE GOSPEL OF JOHN

(2)

THE COINHERENCE OF THE FATHER, THE SON, AND THE SPIRIT

On the surface John 14:16-20, 23, and 26 seem to be easy to understand, but actually these verses contain a very critical truth. These few verses give us a clear revelation concerning the three of the Divine Trinity—the Father, the Son, and the Spirit, showing that the three coinhere and are inseparable.

In John 14:10 the Lord said, "I am in the Father and the Father is in Me," indicating that He and the Father coinhere. However, in verse 16a He said, "And I will ask the Father, and He will give you another Comforter," seeming to imply that He was one person and the Father was another person. This is difficult to understand. First He said that He was in the Father and the Father was in Him, and then He said that He would "ask the Father." What did He mean? How would He ask the Father? Is it that He as the Son who is in the Father would ask the Father? Or is it that He as the Son would ask the Father who is in the Son? This is really difficult to explain and not so easy to understand. How can the Son ask someone a question if that One is in Him and He is in that One? Since the two—the Son and the Father—were already mingled as one, how could the Son ask the Father a question? From this we see that the Son and the Father are two yet one, one yet two.

"Another Comforter"

In verse 16b the Lord went on to say, "And He will give you

another Comforter." Since there would be another Comforter, this means that the Lord Himself, who was with the disciples at that time, was the first Comforter. Are there then two Comforters? Verse 17 says that the other Comforter is "the Spirit of reality, whom the world cannot receive, because it does not behold Him or know Him; but you know Him, because He abides with you and shall be in you." The "Him" referred to in this verse was "another Comforter," while the Lord who spoke this word was the first Comforter, and the One who would abide with the disciples and would be in them was referred to as "Him"—another Comforter. But verse 18 then says, "I will not leave you as orphans; I am coming to you." Here I would ask, When the Lord said that He was coming to His disciples, what did He mean by "coming"? Was He referring to His second coming? If this was the case, then He would be leaving them as orphans. But if so, how could He say that He would not leave them as orphans and that He was coming to them? What does this "coming" refer to?

In the beginning of chapter fourteen the Lord Jesus told the disciples, "I go to prepare a place for you" (v. 2b). This going refers to the Lord's going through death. This is why the disciples were sorrowful when they heard this. Due to their sorrow, the Lord spoke a word to comfort them. In verse 18 the Lord seemed to be saying, "Do not be sorrowful, because soon after I go, I will come back. If I went and did not come back, I would be leaving you as orphans. However, I will not leave you as orphans; I am coming to you." Many teachers in Christianity think that the "coming" in verse 18 refers to the second coming of the Lord. This would mean that at least two thousand years after His going away, He has still not come back and we are still waiting. According to this interpretation, the Lord Jesus has in fact left those who have believed into Him as orphans. This understanding does not match what the Lord meant in these verses.

The World Beholding Him No Longer, but Those Who Believe into Him Beholding Him

In verse 19a the Lord explained, saying, "Yet a little while and the world beholds Me no longer." A *little while* indicates that the Lord's coming mentioned in verse 18 could not be two thousand years later and therefore does not refer to His second coming. *The world beholds Me no longer* implies that He would become invisible, that He would be transfigured. When He was on earth, He was visible to people; regardless of whether they believed in Him or not, whether they approved of Him or opposed Him, all could behold Him. Yet in a little while He would be transfigured and would become invisible to the world. However, verse 19b says, "But you behold Me; because I live, you also shall live." This is very wonderful. Why is it that the world could behold Him no longer, but those who believe into Him could behold Him? It is because He lives, and therefore all those who believe into Him also will live.

The phrase *because I live, you also shall live* means that the Lord lives with us and we with Him. We can see from the New Testament revelation that *I live* refers to the Lord's living in us, and *you also shall live* refers to our living in the Lord. This matches what Paul said: "It is no longer I who live, but it is Christ who lives in me" (Gal. 2:20). Today Christ is living in us, and we are living in Him. The world beholds Him no longer, but we behold Him, because He lives with us; not only so, He lives in us, and we live in Him. Although people cannot see Him without, we can see Him within.

His Coming in Resurrection

John 14:19 implies that the Lord's coming would be in resurrection. If He did not come in resurrection, how could He live in us? Moreover, the Lord's going was His going through death. Since He had gone and had died, how could He still live? This proves that verse 19 implies resurrection. It is true that He went and died, but He was resurrected and could therefore come and live. For that reason, we know that His "coming" refers to His coming in resurrection.

According to this, "a little while" was actually less than three days. After He spoke this word, He was betrayed, arrested, and judged. On the same day He was crucified, and six hours later He expired. That was almost the end of the day, so it is also counted as one day. He stayed in the tomb for a little over twenty-four hours and was resurrected early in the morning of the third day. So if we add the few hours before and after, He went away for probably only a little over thirty hours. Then in the evening of the day of resurrection He came back. This may be likened to a mother who is about to leave home; in order to make her children feel at peace, she tells them that she will not leave them as orphans but will only be gone for a little while and will come back right away. In the same way, the Lord came back after being gone for only "a little while," for only around thirty hours.

According to the calendar of the Jews, a day began at six o'clock in the evening and lasted until six o'clock in the evening of the next day. The Lord spoke the words in John 14 through 16 to His disciples during the evening of the Feast of Passover. Afterward, deep in the night He went to the Garden of Gethsemane. There He was betrayed, arrested, and brought to be judged by the high priest through the night. After being judged, He was sent to Pilate; at that time it was already early morning (18:28). When Pilate heard that the Lord Jesus was a Galilean and was under Herod's jurisdiction, he sent Him to Herod, who was in Jerusalem at that time. However, because the Lord would not answer anything under Herod's questioning, He was sent back to Pilate (Luke 23:6-12). Pilate questioned the Lord Jesus; then he sent Him to be crucified starting at nine o'clock in the morning (Mark 15:25). The Lord suffered on the cross for six hours and expired at three o'clock in the afternoon. When evening fell, Joseph, who was from Arimathea, came to bury Him. It was then nightfall, and this was the first day.

The second day was the Sabbath (Luke 23:56), and the Lord rested. He stayed in the tomb for not more than two nights. On the third day, that is, in the early morning of the Lord's Day when it was still dark, He had already resurrected (John 20:1). Therefore, "three days" is the Jewish way of counting. The proper way is to say that the Lord's going was from the last three hours of the first day, the day of preparation for the Passover (Matt. 26:19; John 19:14), plus the second day, the Sabbath. Then on the third day, the Lord's Day, when it was still dark, He was resurrected, and in the same evening He came. Thus, from His going to His coming, the time was very short. This is why He said that in a little while the world would behold Him no longer. The priests, the scribes, and the Pharisees would not behold Him, but the disciples would behold Him. This is because through His death and resurrection He became the life-giving Spirit, and as such He breathed Himself into the disciples (20:22).

"In That Day"

On the evening of the day of resurrection, the Lord Jesus came to His disciples and breathed into them the promised Spirit, His very reality. In John 14:20 the Lord said, "In that day you will know that I am in My Father, and you in Me, and I in you." *In that day* refers to the day of the Lord's resurrection, and to *know* is to apprehend, experience, and appreciate. When the Lord was speaking to the disciples, they did not know that they would be in Him because He had not yet dispensed Himself into them. At that time, the Lord could at most let them know that He was in the Father and the Father was in Him. However, "in that day," that is, about thirty hours later, in the day of the Lord's resurrection, the disciples knew that the Lord was not only in the Father but also in them, because the Lord breathed Himself into them (20:22). As a result, they were also in Him. "In that day" all these things were accomplished facts, and they "knew," that is, they apprehended, experienced, and appreciated that the Lord was in the Father, they were in the Lord, and the Lord was in them.

The Son and the Spirit Being One

At the end of John 14:17 the Lord said that the Spirit of reality would come to abide with the disciples and be in the disciples. Then in verse 20 He said that the disciples would be in Him and He in them. After saying in verse 17 that the Spirit of reality would be in the disciples, the Lord went on to say in verse 20 that He would be in the disciples. Then, are "the Spirit of reality" and "the Lord" two? Is it possible that two are living in us? We can all testify in our experience that there is only one who lives in us. If so, then which One is living in us?

The more we speak about whether it is the Father, the

Son, or the Spirit who lives in us, the more puzzled we are according to our limited human mentality. We can only say that we know that these verses tell us about the Father, the Son, and the Spirit, but what we know, we still do not know. Yet if we say that we do not know, it seems also that we do know. It is really hard to say how many persons are the Father, the Son, and the Spirit. If we say They are three, it is hard to explain these few verses. If we say They are not three, it is equally hard to understand. Because the mystery concerning the Divine Trinity is so difficult to understand, the theological way of explaining this is to say that the unique God who is the Father, the Son, and the Spirit is the Triune God. He is three yet one; He is Triune.

The Father and the Son Being One

In John 14:23a the Lord said, "If anyone loves Me, he will keep My word, and My Father will love him." Why did the Lord not say that if anyone would love Him, He would love that one, but instead He said that if anyone would love Him, His Father would love that one? Why is it that when someone loves the Son, the Father gets involved? What kind of a love relationship is this? Moreover, the Lord continued in verse 23b: "And We will come to him and make an abode with him." Here "We" appears, indicating that the Father and the Son are together. What does this mean? This means that the Son—who is loved—is in the Father, and the Father is also in the Son. Hence, if the Lord had said, "If anyone loves Me, I will love Him," He would not have revealed the fact that the Son and the Father are one. Therefore, the Lord said, "If anyone loves Me,...My Father will love him." This proves that when you love the Son, you love the Father also, because the Father is in the Son. At the same time, because the Son is in the Father, the result is that the Father as well as the Son respond to your love by loving you. When the Father loves you, it is the Son loving you in the Father and the Father loving you in the Son. Therefore, you cannot love the Son without involving the Father; when you love the Son, the Father appears. The Father responds by loving you, and when the Father loves you, the Son is brought with Him. Hence, the

Lord said "We," indicating that both the Father and the Son come. They come to make an abode with you.

THE FATHER SENDING THE SPIRIT
IN THE NAME OF THE SON,
AND THE SPIRIT COMING
WITH THE FATHER AND THE SON

In John 14:26, a verse which is even harder to understand than the previous verses we have covered, the Lord said, "But the Comforter, the Holy Spirit, whom the Father will send in My name, He will teach you all things." This verse tells us that the Father sends the Spirit in the Son's name; thus, the Spirit is also in the Son's name. Moreover, when the Father sends in the Son's name, is it the Father who sends or the Son who sends? Suppose you go to the bank to withdraw money in Brother Chang's name. When the teller calls Brother Chang's name, you answer and go forward. At this moment the teller does not care whether you are Brother Lin or Brother Wang but only cares for that "name"—Brother Chang. So you just need to give Brother Chang's seal and passbook to the teller, then you can withdraw money in Brother Chang's name. In this respect, at this time you and Brother Chang are one. Similarly, the Father's sending the Spirit in the Son's name means that the Father and the Son are one; the two are inseparable.

Furthermore, when the Spirit comes, He comes with the Father (cf. 15:26, note 1). In other words, the Spirit comes with the One who sends Him. The One who sends the Spirit is the Father, and the Father is in the Son. Hence, when the Spirit, who is sent, comes with the Father, the Father, being in the Son, comes with the Son. As a result, when the Spirit comes, He comes with the Father and the Son. All three—the Father, the Son, and the Spirit—come.

In order to help us understand this verse, we need to read 14:26 and 15:26 again. In 15:26 the Lord said, "But when the Comforter comes, whom I will send to you from the Father, the Spirit of reality." John 14:26 clearly says that the Father will send the Spirit, yet 15:26 says that the Son will send the Comforter from the Father. This means that both the Son and the Father are the Senders, and the sent One is the Spirit, who is from the Father. Here the word *from* has the sense of "from with" in Greek (see 1:14, note 5). The Spirit of reality, who is sent by the Son from the Father, comes not only from the Father but also with the Father. The Father is the source. When this Spirit comes from the source, He does not leave the source but comes with the source. This Spirit, sent by the Son and coming with the Father, testifies concerning the Son. Therefore, His testimony concerning the Son is a matter of the Triune God. Thus, when the Spirit comes, He comes with the Father and also with the Son; therefore, the One who comes is the Triune God.

GOD BEING THE FATHER, THE SON, AND THE SPIRIT
FOR THE PURPOSE OF ENTERING
INTO HIS CHOSEN PEOPLE

The Gospel of John is a book that we love very much, yet it is also a very mysterious book. In particular, the portion in John 14 concerning the truth of the mystery of the Divine Trinity is not easy to explain.

What is the purpose for God to be triune—the Father, the Son, and the Spirit? It is so that He can enter into us as the Spirit. If God were one and did not have the aspect of being three—the Father, the Son, and the Spirit—He would have no way to reach us and dispense Himself into us. The story of the Trinity, God being triune, is altogether for God to enter into us, His chosen people.

Many Christians have not seen the truth of the Divine Trinity in the Bible. Why does God have to be triune? God does not have to be triune to be worshipped by us. The reason He is triune is that He may work Himself into us. For example, if some wheat wants to enter into us, it must first pass through a process. Of course, we can be like the Lord's disciples and eat raw ears of wheat from the grainfields (Matt. 12:1), but that is not the proper way of eating. It is not proper to eat the ears of wheat because they have not been processed. Instead, we should eat the wheat that has been processed. What is the process that the wheat has to go through? First, a grain of wheat has to be sown into the soil so that ears of wheat can be produced. Then the wheat has to be ground into flour and made into bread or noodles for us to receive. Originally it was wheat, but in order to become our food, it has to be ground into flour and then made into bread or noodles. Hence, both the bread and the noodles are made with flour, and the flour comes from the wheat. This does not mean that once you have the bread, the flour is gone, or that once you have the flour, the wheat is gone. What has happened is that after being processed, the wheat has become flour and has been made into noodles for the purpose of getting into us.

THE DIVINE TRINITY BEING FOR US TO EAT

The above illustration helps us to see that the Father, the Son, and the Spirit are one God—the Triune God—to be our food. This is not man's word but the word of the Bible. John 6 tells us about a little boy who had five barley loaves and who came to the place where Jesus and a great crowd gathered. Eventually, the five barley loaves went into the five thousand people who ate them. Later the Lord said, "I am the bread of life" (v. 35). This means that the barley loaves signify the Lord Himself. Then in chapter twelve the Lord said that He is the grain of wheat (v. 24). He is the wheat, and He is also the bread, for the wheat has to be ground into flour before it can be made into bread. He is the wheat, He is also the flour, and He is even more the bread for us to eat. Therefore, when He is the wheat, He is still the bread, and when He is the bread, He is still the wheat.

THE SIGNIFICANCE OF BREAKING THE BREAD

Eating, drinking, and enjoying the Lord are basic truths in the Bible. When the Lord Jesus established His supper, He took the bread and said, "Take, eat; this is My body" (Matt. 26:26). He also said, "This is My body which is being given for you" (Luke 22:19). The Lord's body, signified by the bread, is the Lord Himself. What the Lord meant was that He would go to the cross and give His body for us to eat. He had not yet gone, but in a short while, at dawn, He would go. Therefore, He gave the bread to the disciples, saying that it was His body and that they should take and eat it. This meant that He wanted them to eat Himself.

However, today many Christians make the breaking of bread a religious ritual. The Catholic Church calls it a "Mass" while the Protestant churches call it "Holy Communion." They do not understand that the real spiritual significance of bread-breaking is that Jesus as the embodiment of God is the bread. He was a grain of wheat which went through a process to become flour and a further process to be made into bread for us to eat. Today when we believe in the Lord Jesus, we eat Him. The One in whom we believe is the processed Triune God, and the One of whom we eat is the processed grain of wheat. The Lord as the processed grain of wheat is the bread, and the processed Triune God is the Spirit.

THE BELIEVERS BECOMING
ONE BREAD, ONE BODY, THROUGH EATING

Today the truth of Christ being the Spirit is crystal clear, but I am afraid that you still do not have a complete comprehension of this matter. Please bear in mind that God's economy, God's dispensing, God's union with us, and God's corporate expression are all included in this truth. Regarding the bread in the Lord's table meeting, we are all clear that the wheat has to be ground into flour, and the flour has to be made into bread before it is ready for us to eat. Christ, who is the Triune God, said that He Himself is the bread of life for us to eat. Our partaking of the bread indicates that we participate in Christ, and as a result, we are all made one, to be His one Body. Therefore, the Bible tells us that although we are many, we are one bread, because we all eat Him (1 Cor. 10:17). This bread is the Body of Christ, which is the church, His one corporate expression.

Therefore, in the story of the Divine Trinity we see God's economy, God's dispensing, and God's union with us. Ultimately, we see that we all become one bread, expressing Christ as the embodiment of the Triune God. This bread, which was originally the individual Christ, has now become the corporate Christ. Christ is the embodiment of the Triune God, the fullness of God, and we all are the expression of the fullness of the Triune God. He is the embodiment and the fullness; we are the expression.

CHRIST AS THE ELEMENT
OF THE CORPORATE BREAD

The wheat is ground into flour, the flour is made into bread, and this bread denotes Christ as the individual bread, which after being eaten by us, constitutes us a corporate bread. What we eat spontaneously becomes what we are. When we eat bread, we spontaneously become bread. Therefore, Paul said that although we are many, we are one Body, one bread. As the one large, corporate bread, we have exactly the same elements as Christ, the individual bread. As the corporate bread, we are just the enlargement of Christ as the individual bread. There is no change in element, and the element is nothing less than Christ Himself.

THE ELEMENTS OF THE ALL-INCLUSIVE CHRIST

Now we will see what the elements of Christ are. The elements of Christ comprise all that the Father is in His divine nature and all the elements that Christ obtained in passing through His process. In other words, Christ possesses both the divine element and the human element. He went through a process not only with the divine and human elements, but He also had many other elements added to Him. He was God incarnated. Thus, incarnation is an element. He passed through thirty-three and a half years of human living. Thus, human living is also an element. When He died on the cross, the elements of His death and the effectiveness of His death were added. When He was resurrected, the elements of His resurrection and the power of His resurrection were added. What He passed through was quite a process. This can be compared to a grain of wheat falling into the ground, dying, sprouting and growing, and finally bearing grains to be ground into powder and made into bread for our enjoyment.

From this we see that Christ Himself has the element of God, the element of man, the element of incarnation, the element of human living, the element of death, and the element of resurrection. Moreover, in His ascension He has obtained the element of ascension. After His ascension He has obtained glory. In His ascension and glorification He has obtained the crown, the throne, and the kingship. All these elements have been added to the all-inclusive Christ of God. Hence, Christ is not merely the Triune God but the processed Triune God. Today, the One in whom we believe is such a One, and the One whom we eat and enjoy is also such a One. He is not merely the Savior who gives us eternal life and the hope of eternal life, but He is also the processed Triune God. Jesus, in whom we believe, is such a One! He is too mysterious, too wonderful, too rich, and too all-inclusive!

CHRIST BECOMING ONE WITH US
BY BECOMING THE SPIRIT

The Bible teaches us that when the Lord Jesus died, we died in Him; when He was buried, we were buried in Him; when He was resurrected, we were resurrected in Him; and when He ascended, we ascended in Him. These four great things—co-death, co-burial, co-resurrection, and co-ascension—are truly marvelous. But how do these four things become our reality? The only way is for this One—with whom we died and were buried, resurrected, and ascended—to become the Spirit to enter into us, so that He and we, we and He are united and joined together. Previously, His death, His burial, His resurrection, and His ascension were merely His own and had nothing to do with us. However, since He became the Spirit, once he enters into us, all that He passed through becomes ours, we become Him in life and in nature (but not in the Godhead), and all these items are related to us.

This is not just to be united but to become one. We are not just united with Christ; we are one with Christ. This is the oneness we have with Christ. Before He became the Spirit, He was He, and we were we, but after He entered into us as the Spirit, He and we have become one. Since He and we are one, His death is our death, His burial is our burial, His resurrection is our resurrection, and His ascension is our ascension. We truly died with Him, were buried with Him, were resurrected with Him, and were ascended with Him. On the day we believed in the Lord Jesus, at the very moment we called on

Him, this pneumatic Christ entered into us, and He and we, we and He, became one. As a result, we died with Him, were buried with Him, were resurrected with Him, and were ascended with Him.

In church history a group of saints involved with the inner-life school saw this matter clearly. However, the Lord has opened us further to see that not only have we died and been buried, resurrected, and ascended with Christ, but we even passed through all the processes with Him, so that whatever He is and has passed through is all ours. As the God in eternity, He passed through incarnation, human living, death, and resurrection. Moreover, He ascended, was enthroned, and obtained glory, kingship, and the kingdom. We are one with such a One. The inner-life people taught us co-death, co-burial, co-resurrection, and co-ascension. Today in the Lord's recovery, however, we not only speak about co-death, co-burial, co-resurrection, and co-ascension, but we also teach that the One whom we have received, whom we have gained, and with whom we have become one is the processed Triune God.

THE PROCESSED TRIUNE GOD
BECOMING ONE WITH US

We cannot overlook these eight verses: John 14:16-20, 23, 26, and 15:26. These eight verses speak of the Triune God who passed through all the processes and enters into us to be one with us. These verses are the basis of the divine revelation that He becomes us and we become Him in His life and in His nature, but not in His Godhead. This revelation includes God's economy, God's dispensing, God's union with us, and God's corporate expression. Today if people ask who you are, you should say, "I am so much, I am so great, I am so mysterious and extensive; I do not know how much I am. I am part of the expression of the processed Triune God." Even the word *expression* cannot fully describe who we are; in fact, we are becoming the very One who is true in life and in nature, but not in the Godhead.

CHAPTER SIX

THE TRUTH OF THE MYSTERY
IN THE GOSPEL OF JOHN

(3)

John 16:12-15 says, "I have yet many things to say to you, but you cannot bear them now. But when He, the Spirit of reality, comes, He will guide you into all the reality; for He will not speak from Himself, but what He hears He will speak; and He will declare to you the things that are coming. He will glorify Me, for He will receive of Mine and will declare it to you. All that the Father has is Mine; for this reason I have said that He receives of Mine and will declare it to you." These four short verses reveal a very mysterious matter—the mystery of the Divine Trinity.

THE ERROR OF CHRISTIANITY

The emphasis of traditional Christianity in expounding these few verses is that the Holy Spirit comes to teach us the truth. Because many of the teachings that Jesus gave His disciples when He was on earth were too profound for them to understand, they had to wait for the Holy Spirit to come and teach them. Most Christian teachers say that in verse 12 *many things* refers to many doctrines, *cannot bear them* means that they could not receive or understand the doctrines, and that because of this the Lord would not teach them anything else. In traditional Christianity, *the Spirit of reality* in verse 13 is rendered as *the Spirit of truth,* and most people interpret *truth* to mean doctrine instead of reality. This is the understanding of these few verses in traditional Christianity.

In actuality, what the Lord said in John 16:12-15 is not

a matter of *understanding* doctrines but a matter of *entering into* reality. He was not concerned about the disciples' being able to understand doctrines or truths, but about their being guided *into all the reality*. The traditional Bible expositors think that this passage is talking about doctrines; actually, this kind of understanding is wrong and misses the mark. For this reason, they cannot enter into the mystery revealed in this passage.

The mystery of this portion is in verse 15: "All that the Father has is Mine; for this reason I have said that He receives of Mine and will declare it to you." The Lord did not say, "All that the Father knows has been made known to Me," because it is not a matter of doctrines; instead, He said, "All that the Father has is Mine," indicating that it is a matter of possessions and riches. As the Heir, He has inherited all that the Father has; all that the Father possesses has become His. In other words, all that the Father has is now His. Hence, this is not a matter of doctrine but a matter of "all that the Father has."

The second half of verse 15 says, "For this reason I have said that He receives of Mine." *He* is the Spirit of reality in verse 13. The phrase *for this reason* is an explanation, indicating that the Spirit of reality would not receive doctrines from the Lord, but rather, all the riches of the Father. *Declare it to you* does not only mean that the Spirit would let the disciples know and understand all that the Father has, but also that the Spirit would transfer, transmit, even transfuse into them all that the Father has. All that the Father possesses has been given to the Son and inherited by the Son. Moreover, now the Spirit of reality receives all these riches from the Son and then transfers, transmits, and even transfuses them into the disciples.

THE FATHER, THE SON, AND THE SPIRIT IN JOHN 16:15

John 16:15 is very mysterious. In this verse we have the Father—"Mine," the Son—"I," and the Spirit—"He." Like Matthew 28:19, this verse speaks of the mystery of the Father, the Son, and the Spirit. However, while Matthew 28:19 is an obvious verse concerning the Father, the Son, and the Spirit,

John 16:15 is a relatively hidden verse and is therefore seldom discussed by expositors.

Actually, John 16:15 and Matthew 28:19 are equally important. Moreover, 2 Corinthians 13:14 says, "The grace of the Lord Jesus Christ and the love of God and the fellowship of the Holy Spirit be with you all." This verse also refers to the Father, the Son, and the Spirit. However, the grace of Christ is mentioned first because it is the subject of 2 Corinthians. Related to the revelation of the Divine Trinity—the Father, the Son, and the Spirit—this verse is also as important as the previous two verses.

THE MYSTERY OF THE TRANSMISSION

What is the mystery in John 16:15? In brief, it is the mystery of transmission. We can use electricity as an illustration to explain this mystery. We all know that electricity has the capability of being transmitted. The prefix *trans* means "over," "across," or "through." For example, at the airport a visitor *in transit* is a passenger who is just passing "through." When electricity is sent over or sent across, we call that the transmission of electricity. Where is the electricity transmitted from? It is transmitted from the power plant. How is it transmitted? It is transmitted by means of electric wires.

Similarly, to be filled with the Spirit is to have the Spirit transmitted into us. When we are filled with the Spirit, what actually happens is that we have the Spirit conducted and transmitted into our spirit. This mystery of the transmission of the Spirit is covered in John 16:15.

The Father Being the Source, and Everything Being Included in Him

It is not easy to explain the mystery of transmission. We have pointed out that among the three of the Trinity—the Father, the Son, and the Spirit—the Father as the source has all the riches. "All that the Father has" includes His riches, His possessions, and His wealth, including love, light, holiness, righteousness, kindness, mercy, power, authority, wisdom, and all other positive things, which are beyond the utterance of our limited language.

Furthermore, in the riches of the Father there is "wrath" but not "temper." This is the "science" of the Bible. We lose our temper, but God does not lose His temper. God only has wrath. There is a difference between these two things. Paul says in Ephesians, "Be angry, yet do not sin" (4:26). When we are angry, we easily lose our temper, and once we lose our temper, we may commit sin easily. God, however, is moved to wrath, but He does not lose His temper. Paul said to those who are fathers, "Fathers, do not provoke your children to anger" (6:4). How does a father provoke his child to anger? He does this by losing his temper in dealing with his child. For example, suppose a child does not go home directly after school; instead, he wanders around and as a result arrives home late. If the father loses his temper and chastises his child, the father will become a defeated father. To lose one's temper in this way is to provoke the child's anger. Provoking children to anger damages them by stirring up their flesh. You may have wrath, but do not lose your temper. We have to distinguish between these two matters. However, it is simply not possible for humans to have wrath and not lose their temper; only the angels can do this. The only way we can have wrath and yet not lose our temper is to actively enjoy God and thereby receive His transmission.

"All that the Father has" is truly rich and exceedingly vast! Consider for example His economy, His good pleasure, and His plan. *Hymns,* #608 has five stanzas: the first stanza concerns the Father, the Son, and the Spirit generally; stanzas 2, 3, and 4 are on the Father, the Son, and the Spirit respectively; and stanza 5 tells of our experience. Stanza 2 says that the Father as the source is rich, that His wealth is inexhaustible, and that He is indeed a treasure-store. All these riches and wealth are actually the "all," which has been given to the Son.

The Father Giving All to the Son

In the Gospel of John, the word *all* is used several times. In theology, there are four terms: *all men, all matters, all things,* and *all. All* comprises all matters and all things, and *all things* includes all men. Take Acts 10:34-36 as an example. In the house of Cornelius, Peter said that the Lord Jesus is the Lord of "all." Although The Mandarin Union Version also translates this word as "all," here *all* refers to all men (cf. 1 Tim. 2:4). Peter thought that the Lord was just the Lord of the Jews but not of the Gentiles; however, now when he came to the house of a Gentile, he clearly saw that the Lord was the Lord of all men. Thus, we can see that in this verse *all* refers to *all men*.

In the Gospel of John, the first time the word *all* is mentioned is in 1:3. There the Greek word for *all things* is actually the word for *all*, which includes all men. The second time is in 3:31, which says, "He who comes from above is above all." Verse 35 continues, "The Father loves the Son and has given all into His hand." John 3:35 is a very precious verse. It says that the Father loves the Son and has given all into His hand. Here *all* equals *all that the Father has* in 16:15. Thus, these two verses are joined together. John 3:35 says, "The Father loves the Son and has given all into His hand," and in 16:15 the Lord said, "All that the Father has is Mine." All that the Father has is the Son's because the Father loves the Son and has given all to Him. Moreover, 13:3 says, "Jesus, knowing that the Father had given all into His hands." This verse has the same meaning as 3:35, saying that the Father has given all to the Son. Thus, in 16:15 the Son could say, "All that the Father has is Mine." He said this word based on 3:35 and 13:3, which say that the Father has given all to Him.

The word *given* in 3:35 and 13:3 actually means "transmitted," indicating that the Father's riches have all been transmitted to the Son. All the riches of the Father have been given, transmitted, by the Father to the Son. Moreover, we must see that when the Father transmits all to the Son, the Father also comes with what He transmits. The Father is always in the transmission. This is the first step of the transmission.

All the Fullness of the Godhead Dwelling in Christ Bodily

Paul told us in his Epistles that Christ the Son is the One

in whom all the fullness of the Godhead dwells bodily (Col. 2:9). *Fullness* here is the expression of riches. The full expression of all the riches of the Godhead dwells in Christ bodily. Before His incarnation Christ as the Word of God did not have a physical body. In His incarnation He became a man with a human body. As a man Christ's physical body is His very person, and in Him all the fullness of the Godhead is hidden. This is because the Godhead includes the Father, and since the Father has given all to the Son, the Son is the treasury of all the riches of the Father. Moreover, now that the Son has become flesh, all the riches of the Father spontaneously dwell in the Son bodily. This "dwelling" is the second step of the transmission.

All That the Son Has Being in the Spirit

The third step is that all that the Son has and all that He has obtained have all been transmitted to the Spirit. John 16:15 says, "He receives of Mine." The Spirit has received everything from the Son; all that the Father has was transmitted to the Son, and now all that the Son has, has been transmitted to and received by the Spirit. This is the third step of the transmission.

ALL THAT THE FATHER, THE SON, AND THE SPIRIT HAVE BEING TRANSMITTED TO US BY THE SPIRIT

After receiving all that the Son has, the Spirit comes to "declare" it to us. This means that He comes to transmit it to us. What does the Spirit do when He comes? He transmits to us all that He has received from the Son. This means that all that the Father, the Son, and the Spirit have are all conveyed and transmitted into us by the Spirit.

Our Christian living is often like a car that does not start. This is because we have not received enough transmission of the Spirit. Our "battery" is frequently in a low condition, so our engine does not start. Often when we want to pray, we lack the energy because we do not have the Spirit as the motivating power in us. At such a time we need the transmission of the Spirit; we need the Spirit to be transmitted into our spirit and to fill us.

In John 16:15 we have "Father," "I," "He," and "you." "Father" is the Father, "I" refers to the Son, "He" refers to the Spirit, and "you" refers to us. Therefore, in this verse four persons are mentioned: the Father, the Son, the Spirit, and us. The riches in the Father are transmitted into the Son; then all that is in the Son is transmitted into the Spirit of reality; finally when the Spirit of reality comes, He transmits into us all that He has obtained and all that He possesses.

The Father, the Son, and the Spirit are mysterious yet very simple. In contrast, human beings are very complicated. The Lord Jesus was God, yet He became a man—a complicated man. Do not think that we are simple. In fact, it seems that the more spiritual we are, the more complicated we become. If you love the world and commit sin, this is very simple, because there is nothing but darkness in you, and you are totally in darkness and are earthly. But once you believe in the Lord Jesus, it seems you become quite "unclear." You do not know whether you are in heaven, on the earth, or in the air. Even you yourself cannot clearly describe your situation. Sometimes you feel that you are full of the Holy Spirit and full of life, and other times you feel that you are heavenly and uplifted. Most of the time, however, you feel that you are so muddled and entirely earthly. The reason we are so complicated is that we are earthly people by nature, but we also have the Spirit within us. Once the Spirit comes into us, He brings the heavens to us; the Spirit and the heavens are very close. However, if there is not enough transmission of the Spirit within us, then we are far away from the heavens and close to the earth.

Thus, you see that there is a wonderful transmitting, a wonderful conveying, in this universe. You may say that it is "the transmitting of the Spirit," "the transmitting of the Lord," "the transmitting of God," or "the transmitting of the heavens." In short, it is simply the transmitting of the Triune God into us. Consequently, we become people who are of the Spirit, who are of the Lord, who are of God, and who are of the heavens. This is the spiritual significance of the "transmission."

THE DIVINE DISPENSING OF THE DIVINE TRINITY

In order to receive the divine transmission, every morning we must spend time to contact the Lord. As a result, we will have the motivating power for the whole day. For example, if you want to take a trip by car, especially a long trip, the safest thing to do is to go to the gas station first to have the car filled up with gasoline and to make sure your battery is fully charged with electricity. In like manner, every day we need to be "filled up with gas" and "charged with electricity." What is the "gas" with which we are filled? And what is the "electricity" with which we are charged? John 16:15 shows us that we need to have the Triune God added to us and transmitted into us. This transmission is the divine dispensing of the Divine Trinity.

BEING A CORPORATE EXPRESSION

Once the Father, the Son, and the Spirit are dispensed into us, They are mingled with us and become one with us. For example, there are twenty to thirty fluorescent lamps in the meeting hall. Once the electricity is transmitted, all the lamps light up. Outwardly, there are twenty to thirty lamps, but inwardly there is only one flow of electricity. The lamps are many, but the electricity is one. Moreover, there is only one shining and one light. Therefore, the twenty to thirty lamps have only one flow of electricity and give out only one light. This is a corporate expression.

If there is only one lamp in the room, although it may shine, the shining is not corporate but individual. There is only one lamp, one flow of electricity within, and one shining without. The electricity in the lamp, the lamp itself, and the illumination of the lamp are all one. This is an individual expression. This was the situation when the Lord Jesus was on the earth. He was an individual "lamp," and His shining on people and His expression of God were both individual. However, today, as His multiplication, we are thousands and millions of "Jesuses," thousands and millions of "lamps." Yet the "electricity" within is still one and the "shining" without is also one. This is a corporate expression.

Stanza 3 of *Hymns,* #501 says, "All things of the Father are Thine; / All Thou art in Spirit is mine; / The Spirit makes Thee real to me, / That Thou experienced might be." This stanza, which is written exactly according to John 16:15, says that all that the Father has is given to and received by the Son; all that the Son has received and all that He has is in the Spirit; the Spirit makes the Son real to us by entering into us; and as a result, this reality may become our experience. This means that if we listen to many messages concerning Christ, the Son, but do not have the Spirit of reality coming into us, none of the messages will be reality. When the Spirit comes into our spirit, this is the coming of the reality of the Son, and the result is that this reality becomes our experience. This may be considered the best explanation of John 16:15.

CHAPTER SEVEN

THE DIVINE DISPENSING IN THE BOOK OF EPHESIANS

THE DIVINE TRINITY BEING THE CONSTITUENT OF THE BOOK OF EPHESIANS

Ephesians is a wonderful book on the divine dispensing. In the entire Bible, Ephesians is the only book in which every chapter is structured with the Divine Trinity as its basic element. For example, chapter one speaks about the Father's selection and predestination, the Son's redemption, and the Spirit's sealing and pledging. This is the basic element of the structure of Ephesians 1.

The Divine Trinity in Chapter One for the Accomplishment of God's Economy

Ephesians 1 reveals that the Father selected and predestinated us before the foundation of the world according to His plan. In time the Son redeemed us for accomplishing what the Father had planned, and after the Son accomplished redemption, the Spirit came to seal us and be a pledge to us for the application of what the Son accomplished. Hence, the Son accomplished all that the Father planned, and after the Son accomplished redemption, the Spirit applies all that the Son has accomplished to us. This is the constitution of chapter one, which is on the accomplishment of God's economy. In other words, the accomplishment of God's redemption and salvation depends entirely on the Divine Trinity—the Father, the Son, and the Spirit.

The Divine Trinity in Chapter Two for Leading Us into the Triune God

In chapter two the Divine Trinity is not as clearly and

distinctly referred to as in chapter one, but in 2:18 the Trinity is implied—"For through Him we both have access in one Spirit unto the Father." This shows us that the Father as the source is the One who predestinates and plans. How do we have access to the Father? First, it is through the Son, who, by accomplishing redemption, became the means by which we have access unto the Father. Second, to have access to the Father we need to be in the Spirit. If we have the means but not the leading, we still cannot reach the goal. Therefore, this verse points out concisely and accurately that we have access unto the Father through the Son, who accomplished redemption, and in the Spirit, who is the sealing and leading; that is, through the Son we have access in one Spirit unto the Father. As a result we, the created, fallen, and redeemed human beings, have been brought together with the Triune God. In other words, we have been wrought into Him.

THE CHURCH—THE CORPORATE EXPRESSION OF GOD

Ephesians chapter one speaks a great deal concerning the Triune God. The central thought is that the Triune God has wrought Himself into us through His selection, predestination, redemption, sealing, and pledging. Chapter two says that through the Son and in the Spirit we have access unto the Father, that is, we enter into the Father. Hence, chapter one reveals that God has come into us, while chapter two tells us that we have entered into the Father. Through this coming and going, the Triune God has wrought Himself into us and us into Him. Thus, we have the economy of God, the dispensing of God, and the union of God with us, resulting in the producing of the Body, the church. The church is the issue of God's coming into us and our going back to Him. Through this coming and going the church as God's corporate expression is produced.

This is a fundamental truth in the Lord's recovery: the Triune God—the Father, the Son, and the Spirit—has wrought Himself into us through the Father's predestination, the Son's redemption, and the Spirit's sealing and pledging. Since we were redeemed and have the Triune God in us, through the Son we have access in the Spirit unto the Father. Through this coming and going, the Triune God has entered into us, and we have also entered into Him; the result is that a corporate expression—the church, the Body of Christ—is produced.

Paul's Prayer in Ephesians 3

In chapter three we see a very deep relationship and union, as well as a profound transmission, dispensing, and mingling between the Triune God and us. Verses 14 to 19 say, "For this cause I bow my knees unto the Father, of whom every family in the heavens and on earth is named, that He would grant you, according to the riches of His glory, to be strengthened with power through His Spirit into the inner man, that Christ may make His home in your hearts through faith, that you, being rooted and grounded in love, may be full of strength to apprehend with all the saints what the breadth and length and height and depth are and to know the knowledge-surpassing love of Christ, that you may be filled unto all the fullness of God." In these few verses the emphasis is on the Father, the Spirit, and Christ. In chapter one it is on the Father, the Son, and the Spirit; in chapter two it is on the Son, the Spirit, and the Father; and in chapter three it is on the Father, the Spirit, and Christ (the Son). Both the sequence and the emphasis are clearly revealed in these chapters.

In chapter three the Father is the source; He initiates, directs, and manages. Recognizing Him as the One who initiates, directs, and manages, the apostle Paul prayed to Him. In so doing, he took the right way and found the right door; he came before the Initiator, Director, and Manager and solemnly knelt down in prayer. This is not a small thing.

We all know that we can pray at any time, in any place, and in any posture. We can pray while we are standing, lying down, stooping, or in any posture we like. However, of all the different postures, the most solemn one is to bow our knees. There is nothing special in simply kneeling down, but to bow our knees, however, is to kneel down in a solemn way. In the Bible, when God's people pray to Him, the most solemn posture is to bow their knees. Bowing our knees means we humble our whole being before God and pray in a solemn way.

Asking the Father according to His Glory

What did Paul ask for when he prayed in such a solemn way? We can see that he asked the Father to do something according to His glory. This is an immensely great matter! I have been meeting with the church and the saints for almost sixty years, and I have heard many, many prayers, but I have never heard a prayer asking God to do things according to His glory. Today whenever we meet, we have prayer; almost every time we gather together, we pray. Moreover, we encourage everyone to pray by himself. However, have we ever prayed, "Lord, I pray that You would raise up the small groups according to Your glory. Lord, establish the home meetings according to Your glory"?

Most of the time when we pray, we ask the Lord to do something according to His grace. Sometimes we are somewhat humble, so we may ask Him according to His mercy; at other times we are very close to Him, so we may ask Him according to His great love. Sometimes we may want to say something that sounds nicer, so we ask Him according to His holiness; other times we see something unpleasant and become angry, so we may ask Him according to His righteousness and justice; and sometimes we pay attention to power, so we may ask the Lord according to His power. We probably have prayed to the Lord in all of these ways, but have we ever prayed according to His glory? I am afraid not. It is even doubtful that there is such a prayer anywhere on the earth today. The reason is that man does not have adequate knowledge of the glory of God.

According to the Bible, the glory of God is God expressed in His divine life and nature. For example, when a flower blossoms, it is glorified. In the same way, when God is expressed, He is glorified. In this sense, what Paul meant when he prayed "according to His glory" is: "Father, may You do things according to Your intention to have Yourself expressed!" Hence, Paul's prayer is related to the dispensing and mingling of the Triune God for the purpose of obtaining a corporate expression of Himself. This corporate expression is the Father's glory, and it was according to this glory that Paul prayed to God.

The Glorification of the Lord Being
the Bearing of Much Fruit

The glory of God is truly a great topic. In His thirty years of human living and three and a half years of ministry, the Lord gave many profound and excellent messages. Among them, there are two that are most impressive and delightful. One is in Matthew 5—7, the teaching on the mountain concerning the truth of the kingdom; the other is in John 14—16, the Lord's speaking to His disciples on the night that He was betrayed concerning the mystery of the union of the Triune God with His believers. Before He was going to speak this long final message, He had already referred to glory several times. For example, in John 12:23 He said, "The hour has come for the Son of Man to be glorified," and in verse 28 He prayed, "Father, glorify Your name." Thus, in His speaking and in His prayer He had already referred to glory.

Following this, in chapter thirteen before Judas went out, the Lord pointed out that Judas was going to betray Him, and gave him a morsel. Most Bible readers do not understand this. They think that the Lord's dipping the morsel and giving it to Judas was a sign to let the disciples know that Judas was the one who would betray the Lord. However, that was not what the Lord intended to do. The Lord's intention was to send Judas to betray Him; for the Lord also said to him, "What you do, do quickly." The Lord seemed to say, "Are you going to betray Me? Now the hour has come; go and betray Me." What was the hour that had come? In 12:23 the Lord said, "The hour has come for the Son of Man to be glorified." This was the hour, so the Lord asked Judas to do what he was going to do. Thus, having taken the morsel, Judas went out. Immediately after that, the Lord said, "Now has the Son of Man been glorified, and God has been glorified in Him. If God has been glorified in Him, God will also glorify Him in Himself, and He will glorify Him immediately" (13:31-32). What the Lord meant was that Judas would go to betray Him and that He was very happy, because as a result He would be glorified.

From this we can see clearly what glory is. In fact, we can

say that the subject of John 12 and 13 is the unveiling of God's glorification of Christ with His glory and the issue of the glorification of Christ through His death and resurrection—a grain of wheat producing many grains (12:24). To the Lord, glory is His being sown as a grain of wheat into the ground as a result of Judas' betrayal. When men killed and buried the Lord, they sowed the Lord into the ground. However, when the Lord was sown into the ground as a grain of wheat, that was not His end. As the grain sown into the ground, the Lord died, but as a result He bore much fruit; this "much fruit" is His glory. The life of God, the element of God, and everything of God that was originally in the Son are now expressed through His becoming the many grains. This is glory.

After Judas went out, the Lord said, "Now has the Son of Man been glorified" (13:31). Following this, He spoke the message in John 14 through 16 to the disciples. Then after this speaking, at the very beginning of chapter seventeen He prayed, "Father, the hour has come; glorify Your Son that the Son may glorify You" (v. 1). When He prayed this, what He meant was, "O Father, may You accomplish this matter. Let them arrest Me, put Me on the cross, and bury Me, for only then can I be resurrected and glorified, and You can also be glorified!" This is the Father glorifying the Son that the Son may glorify the Father.

Removing the Veils Which Hinder the Glory from Being Expressed

This glory was fully expressed in the Lord Jesus, but it has not yet been fully expressed through us today. God has already wrought Himself into us, and He desires to be lived out from us. Sadly, however, He has been "detained" in us and has no way to come out. Our self, our natural man, our flesh, our temperament, our disposition, our habits, our opinions, our insight, and our preferences have become factors that hinder the release of the divine glory. Our sins, trespasses, and covetousness are not the only obstacles to the expression of the divine glory, but even the brothers' inappropriate shirts and ties and the sisters' improper hairstyles and adornment are as well.

This kind of speaking is not too much. I know too well the story of the young people. For example, when the sisters enter into the department stores, they are totally disarmed and defeated. Not to mention how they were in the past, even after being saved they still buy many things that the Lord does not want them to buy. Even though they know clearly that the Lord does not want them to buy those things, they still give the Lord many excuses, such as, "It is on sale"; "I will regret it if I do not get it"; and "It is going out of stock." Eventually, they buy everything. We all have to confess that too many times we refuse to do what the Lord wants us to do; instead, we do all the things that the Lord forbids. If this is the case, how can the Lord be glorified from within us? How can He be expressed through us?

I would like you to know that people in business put out advertisements so that they can transfer other people's money into their own pockets. Therefore, when the sisters go shopping, they should buy things only according to their need and the Lord's leading. They should not be influenced by the advertisements. Whenever we do things according to our own desire instead of according to the Lord's leading, we are covered by a layer of veils. Every time we are covered with one more layer, until layer after layer the veils become so thick that the glory within us has no way to be expressed. How many times today, not to mention in the past or even in our entire history since being saved, did we go ahead and do something, big or small, that we clearly knew the Lord did not want us to do? And how many times did we know clearly that the Lord wanted us to do something, yet we would not do it? If during the course of one day we have been covered by so many layers of veils, how can the Lord be expressed through us?

In light of our condition, Paul asked the Father to work according to His glory. This means that he asked the Father to remove the veils layer by layer from within us. Many Bible readers acknowledge that Paul had a very high level of scholastic ability in Greek. When he wrote the book of Ephesians, he used the Greek language to the fullest extent. Paul prayed to the Father "according to the riches of His glory"; in Greek, this means that the glory of the Father is not poor but rich and unsearchable. He asked the Father to work according to the riches of His glory so that the Triune God may be expressed from within us.

Being Strengthened with Power through His Spirit

Moreover, Paul asked the Father to grant us to be strengthened with power through His Spirit into our inner man. Our inner man is our regenerated spirit, which has God's life as its life and is indwelt by the Holy Spirit. It is also our new person.

Our inner man, in brief, is our regenerated spirit. Consider how much you remain in your spirit every day. Psychologists classify human beings, according to human disposition, as introverts and extroverts. A so-called introvert is a person whose interest is not in the things outside of him but in the things within himself; he does not like to talk and does not have much to say. A so-called extrovert is a person whose interest is more on the things outside of him than on the things within himself; he likes to talk and has many things to say. Actually, the "inner man" referred to in the Bible is the real "introvert." In the biblical sense, a person is an "extrovert" regardless of whether he speaks much or speaks little; only when he turns to his spirit is he truly an "introvert." Many times it requires the combined strength of nine oxen and two tigers for us to return to our spirit. Sometimes even in the meetings we are not in our spirit, and it usually takes us half an hour to return to our spirit.

Ephesians 3:16 is really profound and hard to comprehend. Paul prayed for us to be strengthened into the inner man and not to remain in the outer man. When you talk endlessly, surely you are in your outer man, yet even when you sit in meditation without praying or fellowshipping, you are in your mind and are therefore still in your outer man, not in your inner man. It is hard to comprehend the difference between the outer man and the inner man, and we often mistake one for the other.

For this reason, Paul prayed that the Father would grant us to be strengthened, in particular to be strengthened into our inner man. When we are weak, obviously we are in our outer man. In the meetings once we criticize, judge, or despise others, this proves that we are weak. Yet even if we do not criticize, judge, or despise others, merely sitting in the meeting without functioning, having no strength to pray or call on the Lord also shows that we are weak. At this time we really need the Spirit to strengthen us. Who directs the Spirit to strengthen us? It is the Father; He initiates, directs, and manages, causing the Spirit to stir us up and fan us into flame.

We all have the experience of being weak most of the time. Even though we know that the Lord does not want us to buy a certain thing, we still buy it. When we pick up something in the department store, and the Lord tells us to put it down, we just cannot put it down. The strangest thing is that we have the strength to pick it up, but do not have the strength to put it down; we are strong to pick it up, but we are weak to put it down. However, sometimes we also have another kind of experience. While we are struggling, suddenly there is a surge of strength within us, so that we are able to put the item down and leave without saying a word. I believe that this is the effect of Paul's prayer. Not only so, many times when you are about to quarrel with your spouse or argue with another believer, you begin to say something and suddenly stop half way. This is because you have been strengthened into your spirit. Then you go back to your room and pray, "Lord, forgive me, because I almost acted out of my flesh. Thank You for being merciful to me and preserving me." This is the Spirit strengthening you from within. Once you are strengthened, you are able to enter into your inner man.

Christ Making His Home
in Our Hearts through Faith That
We May Be Rooted and Grounded in Love

Paul used the word *that* repeatedly in Ephesians 3; he used it four times in verses 16-19 alone. The first time he used it is in verse 16 when he prayed *that* the Father would grant us "to be strengthened with power through His Spirit into the inner man." The second time, in verse 17a, he said,

"That Christ may make His home in your hearts through faith." The third time, in verses 17b-19a, he said, *"That* you...may be full of strength to apprehend...and to know the...love of Christ." The fourth time, in verse 19b, he said, *"That* you may be filled unto all the fullness of God." In these verses the word *that* may also be translated as *in order that,* meaning that the second *that* is the result of the first *that,* the third *that* is the result of the second *that,* and so forth.

Verse 17 says, "That Christ may make His home in your hearts through faith, that you, being rooted and grounded in love." This is the result of our being strengthened into the inner man (v. 16). What does it mean for Christ to make home? Making home has a deeper meaning than staying in a certain place; it does not merely mean to stay somewhere but to settle down there. Christ is in you, but He may be like a guest merely sitting in a chair, leaning against the wall, or standing in the corner. However, once your whole being is strengthened into your spirit, He has the ground and the right to settle down and make home in you. For example, suppose I am moving to a new house, but the original owner will not vacate the house. If this is the case, I will not know where to put my furniture; the most I can do is to put it in the living room. Not until the house is empty will I be able to unpack and put everything in order, thus, making home and settling down there.

Has Christ settled down and made His home in us? Sometimes He is at home within us but sometimes He is not, because we often struggle with Him. When we are joyful, we may pray, "Lord, I love You." However, we should not think that we have prayed well and that this is enough, because when we struggle with Him, we may not love Him anymore. Sometimes when we struggle with the Lord, we may even force Him into a corner. Although He comes back again a few days later, we do not have peace in our spirit because we always have this kind of struggle within. Before we were saved, we may have seemed to be at peace all the time. If we wanted to scold someone, we would just do it, and we were very happy after doing it; we were free to do whatever our heart dictated.

But after we became a Christian, even the thought of blaming others, let alone scolding them, causes us to have no peace within, because it interrupts the Lord's making His home in us. Once He is prevented from making His home in us, He does not have peace, and we also do not have peace.

In Matthew 11:28 the Lord Jesus said, "Come to Me all who toil and are burdened, and I will give you rest." When I was young, even before I was saved, I had already heard this word being preached, and I also loved to preach it to people. Now when I think back, I realize that I simply did not know what I was talking about. The only way for you to genuinely receive rest from the Lord is to let Him make His home in you. If you do not let the Lord make His home in you, it will not be possible for you to find rest. The rest which the Lord gives is His making home in you. If you let Him settle down in you peacefully, you will be blessed. However, today among thousands and millions of Christians, it is rare to find one or two who are willing to let the Lord make His home and settle down in them.

In order to let the Lord make His home and settle down in us, we need both faith and love (1 Tim. 1:14). Through faith we apprehend Christ, and through love we enjoy Christ. However, neither faith nor love is from us; both are from Christ. For this reason, we need to be strengthened into our inner man. In this way, His faith becomes our faith, enabling us to believe Him, and His love becomes our love, enabling us to love Him. When we are rooted and grounded in Christ's love, we grow in life and are built up in His life.

Apprehending the Breadth,
Length, Height, and Depth of Christ

Once the Lord has made His home in our hearts, Paul continued to say, the result is that we are "full of strength to apprehend with all the saints what the breadth and length and height and depth are" (Eph. 3:18). Here the breadth, length, height, and depth refer to the breadth, length, height, and depth of the universe. Who can tell how wide is the breadth, how long is the length, how high is the height, and how deep is the depth of the universe? We all know that many, many solar systems constitute one galaxy, and many, many galaxies constitute the universe. The universe is boundless, and its breadth, length, height, and depth are also limitless. These dimensions are the dimensions of Christ; Christ is such an unlimited One. When Christ makes His home in our hearts for us to experience and enjoy, we find that this Christ, into whom we believe and whom we enjoy, know, and experience, is boundless and unsearchable.

Knowing the Knowledge-surpassing Love of Christ in Our Experience

Verse 19a says, "And to know the knowledge-surpassing love of Christ." According to the context, this means that due to the Lord's making His home in us, we can experience Him as the unsearchable One. Immediately we can also know His love; that is, we know that His love surpasses human knowledge and understanding. It is very strange that on the one hand, Christ's love surpasses human understanding, but on the other hand, we can know it. Man can neither know nor understand this love, yet we who allow the Lord to make His home in us can know and experience it. According to our intellect, Christ's love is knowledge-surpassing, and our mind can never understand it; according to our experience in our spirit, however, we can know it.

Once we experience Christ's making His home in us, we can know how great the love of Christ is. That the Triune God would make us His dwelling place and would reside in us to be our life, our nature, and our content reveals the greatness of the love of Christ. What a love this is! How great a love this is! This is not only the love in His dying on the cross for us but also the love in His entering into us. How excellent the heavens are, and how beautiful the earth is! Yet the Lord is not satisfied; rather, He longs to dwell in us, making us His home, that He may be our life and nature and become our content. Can we imagine what kind of great love this is?

Throughout the centuries very few Christians have apprehended Christ's love to such an extent. The majority of Christians know only the Lord's love in dying on the cross for them; they do not know His love in His making His home in them. He loves us to the extent that He not only died for us but also considers us His dwelling place. Who are we? How uncomely we are! Yet He comes to make His home in us, to be our life, our nature, and our content, and to live and move in us. Hence, it is not until we allow Christ to make His home in us that we will be able to understand the extent of the Lord's love toward us and to know His knowledge-surpassing love.

Being Filled unto the Fullness of the Triune God

Verse 19b says, "That you may be filled unto all the fullness of God." In the preceding verses Paul referred to the mystery of the Divine Trinity: he prayed that the Father would grant us to be strengthened with power through His Spirit into our inner man, that Christ the Son may make His home in our hearts, and that we would be filled unto all the fullness of God—unto the expression of all the riches of God. This is not merely the fullness of the Father, nor of the Son, nor of the Spirit; this is the fullness of God, the fullness of the Divine Trinity. How wonderful! How glorious! This is an outline of Ephesians 3, a chapter which is full of the divine dispensing, transmission, union, and mingling, and ultimately the accomplishing of God's economy and the producing of a corporate expression.

THE TRIUNE GOD IN EPHESIANS 4

In chapter four we see the Spirit, the Lord, and the Father. In chapter one, it is the Father, the Son, and the Spirit; in chapter two, it is the Son, the Spirit, and the Father; in chapter three, it is the Father, the Spirit, and the Son; and in chapter four, it is the Spirit, the Son, and the Father. In 4:3-6 Paul mentions seven "ones": one Body, one Spirit, one hope, one Lord, one faith, one baptism, and one God and Father of all. This portion indicates that the Son comes from the Father for us to believe in, to receive, and to enter into, and the result is that we become His Body. The One who dwells in this Body is the Spirit, who is the ultimate manifestation of the Triune God—the Father, the Son, and the Spirit. Hence, the ultimate manifestation of the Father, the Son, and the Spirit dwells in a corporate habitation, which is the Body as the expression of the Triune God.

Now we see that the dispensing of the Divine Trinity issues in the one Body, in which dwells the Spirit as the ultimate manifestation of the Father, the Son, and the Spirit. Moreover, eventually, the Body is the expression of the Father, the Son, and the Spirit. In brief, the Triune God's economy is to dispense and transmit Himself into us, His believers, and to continuously unite and mingle Himself with us that we may become His one Body as His corporate expression.

THE CORPORATE EXPRESSION OF THE TRIUNE GOD

All of us who serve the Lord must see this matter. In all of our messages, words, truths, and preaching, we should take this as the starting point, the content, and the destination. We must show people that according to His economy, the Triune God is working Himself into us—dispensing, transmitting, uniting, and mingling Himself with us—producing the one Body, which includes humanity, divinity, incarnation, human living, death, resurrection, and ascension.

This is a mystery as well as an aggregate. In John 15 this mystery is the universal true vine; furthermore, in chapters twenty-one and twenty-two of Revelation, the last book written by John, the aggregate is the New Jerusalem. In John 15 we see the universal true vine; in Revelation 21—22 the universal true vine is the New Jerusalem. The Triune God is producing an organism through His dispensing, transmitting, uniting, and mingling to express Himself for the accomplishment of His eternal economy.

CHAPTER EIGHT

THE MYSTERY OF THE DIVINE TRINITY IN THE GOSPEL OF MATTHEW

The matter of the Triune God is not a superficial theological doctrine. We need both to believe into and deeply enter into the mystery of the Divine Trinity. In the Bible, the Gospel of John and the book of Ephesians speak clearly about the mystery of the Divine Trinity; the Gospel of Matthew also reveals this divine truth to us.

THE DIVINE TRINITY IN THE GOSPEL OF MATTHEW

Not a Matter of Being "in the Lord's Name," But a Matter of the Mingling of the Triune God with Man

Matthew 28:19, the next to the last verse in the whole book of Matthew, says, "Baptizing them into the name of the Father and of the Son and of the Holy Spirit." Some versions render *into the name* as *in the name*. Many in Christianity quote this verse during baptism, and their reason for doing so is merely to do something "in the name." To the Chinese, to do something in someone's name equals carrying their flag, indicating that you represent that person. Thus, according to this way of thinking, when you do something in the name of the Triune God, it means that you are "carrying the Triune God's flag" and that you are representing Him. For example, when an army is carrying the American flag, even if there are Mexicans in the army, their flag indicates that they are also fighting for America. Another example is that during monarchical times, when a little eunuch came with an imperial order, all the officials, regardless of their rank, had to bow down to receive it; if anyone opposed the order brought by this eunuch, this one was actually opposing the emperor. People in traditional Christianity delight in baptizing people "in the Lord's name," yet they do not know the deeper meaning of Matthew 28:19 concerning the union and mingling of God and man.

After studying the Bible in depth for many years, I have seen that baptizing people *into* the name of the Father, the Son, and the Holy Spirit is far more meaningful than simply baptizing them *in* the name of the Father, the Son, and the Holy Spirit. *Into* indicates union. To baptize people into the name of the Triune God is to bring them into a spiritual and mystical union with the Triune God.

The Triune God in Matthew 1

The Gospel of Matthew refers to the Triune God at the very beginning of the first chapter. Verse 23b has the phrase, "God with us." In what way is God with us? Does this simply mean that although we were on the earth and He was in heaven, one day He came down from heaven to be with us because He loves us? In order to explain this, we must use the Bible to interpret the Bible. First, we need to see how it was that He came and what He did after His coming. The first half of verse 23 says, "The virgin shall be with child and shall bear a son, and they shall call His name Emmanuel." Thus, He came by being conceived of a virgin, and He came also to be *Emmanuel,* which is translated, "God with us."

Now we will go on to see how the virgin conceived a child. Verse 20 says, "For that which has been begotten in her is of the Holy Spirit." This means that One who was of the Holy Spirit had been begotten in Mary. Who is this One? The One who had been begotten in her was God Himself. This is too great a truth. However, almost all the Bible versions, including the Mandarin Union Version, do not translate this verse accurately to show forth this great truth. Most of the translations read, "For that which is conceived in her is of the Holy Spirit." This is nearly the same as what is said in verse 18—"Mary...was found to be with child of the Holy Spirit"—and it is still unclear who was conceived in Mary. In actuality, verse 20 explains verse 18, clearly showing that the One whom she conceived had been begotten in her through the Holy Spirit. Hence, it is not merely a matter of conception, but of begetting, for this verse also indicates that there was One begotten in her. That this One is of the Holy Spirit means that He is out of God and comes from God; God had been begotten in her. Here we can see God and the Holy Spirit.

Verses 21-23 say, "And she will bear a son, and you shall call His name Jesus, for it is He who will save His people from their sins. Now all this has happened so that what was spoken by the Lord through the prophet might be fulfilled, saying, 'Behold, the virgin shall be with child and shall bear a son, and they shall call His name Emmanuel.'" This means that the One who was born of Mary is Jesus as well as Emmanuel. He is one person, yet He has two names. He is Jesus, and this Jesus is Emmanuel. Jesus is a man, yet His name is "Jehovah the Savior." This shows us that the Father has become Emmanuel by passing through the process of the Triune God. This process transpired with the Father entering into a virgin through the Spirit and being born of her with humanity. The One who was born was Jesus—the Son. Who is Jesus? He is God with man. In addition, in the name Jesus, *Je* stands for Jehovah, and *sus* means "Savior" or "salvation." At this point we can see that in Matthew 1 the revelation concerning the Triune God is complete and mysterious.

In brief, in reference to the Triune God, Matthew chapter one says that God is with us and that He becomes Emmanuel. But how can He be with us? And how did He become Emmanuel? The first step is that He was begotten into a human virgin through the Spirit. The second step is that He came out of the human virgin and was born with humanity to be Jesus, who is the Savior, and the Son, who is both the Son of Man and the Son of God. He was actually the Triune God coming as our Savior to save us from our sins. Not only so, the third step is that He comes into us to be with us and to be our life and our all. If we study Matthew 1 carefully, we will see that this chapter is very rich and that it clearly reveals the Triune God at the outset. However, it does not discuss the Triune God as a theological doctrine; rather, it reveals how the Triune

God passed through various processes to be our Savior, saving us from our sins and coming into us.

According to the letter, the story in Matthew 1 is merely about how Mary conceived a child of the Holy Spirit and begot a son, whose name was Jesus and whom people called Emmanuel. It seems that it tells us only this much. When we receive revelation, however, we will see that this chapter tells us that the Triune God has been processed to become our Savior, who saves us from our sins and comes into us to be our life and our all for the accomplishment of God's eternal purpose. We should not study the Bible merely according to the letter without any light or revelation. If we do this, all we will have is merely doctrines in letter. Rather, we need to ask God to give us a Spirit of wisdom and revelation.

The Mystery of the Divine Trinity in Matthew 3

While it is not easy to find references to the Father, the Son, and the Spirit in Matthew 2, the revelation concerning the Divine Trinity in Matthew 3 is very clear. Matthew 3:16-17 says, "And having been baptized, Jesus went up immediately from the water, and behold, the heavens were opened to Him, and He saw the Spirit of God descending like a dove and coming upon Him. And behold, a voice out of the heavens, saying, This is My Son, the Beloved, in whom I have found My delight." This portion reveals the Triune God and is a picture of the Divine Trinity—the Son rose up from the water, the Spirit descended upon the Son, and the Father spoke concerning the Son from heaven. This proves that the Father, the Son, and the Spirit exist simultaneously. This is for the accomplishing of God's economy.

Some people in Catholicism and Protestantism conclude that in the picture of the Lord's baptism in Matthew 3, there are obviously three God's in three different places—the Son is standing in the water, the Spirit is descending upon the Son from the air, and the Father is speaking downward from heaven. However, I hope we all can see that although Matthew 3 definitely says that the Father, the Son, and the Spirit are in three different places, John 10 says that the Father is in the Son and the Son is in the Father (v. 38). This verse reveals that They are in one another mutually. Here it is not a matter of location but a matter of existence. This is the way to study the Bible. We must interpret the Bible with the Bible and not solely according to our natural logic.

Perhaps some will ask, "Then, does the Bible contradict itself? Why does Matthew 3 say that there is One in heaven, One in the air, and One in the water, yet John indicates that the three are in one another?" Every matter in the universe has two sides. For example, although the front of my head has seven "holes" and the back has none, this is not a contradiction. Nothing can exist without two sides; even a sheet of paper has its front and its back. Do not try to reconcile the two sides; just look for the facts and acknowledge the facts. Only the blind guides of the blind argue irrationally, grasping one side while forgetting the other.

Then, what is the fact here? The fact is "the Triune God." This term is sufficiently clear in expression. The Triune God is not composed of three Gods; the Triune God is uniquely one but has the aspect of being three. "The Triune God" does not refer to His persons; it refers to the substance of His being. It is not an explanation of His persons but an explanation of the substance of what He is. God is uniquely one, but in substance He is three; thus, He is triune. For this reason, the Bible not only reveals that the Father, the Son, and the Spirit coinhere; it further reveals that the Son is the Father (Isa. 9:6), that the Son became the Spirit (1 Cor. 15:45), and that the Son is the Spirit (2 Cor. 3:17). This is the divine fact, the divine truth.

The Mystery of the Divine Trinity in Matthew 28

By the end of the Gospel of Matthew, chapter twenty-eight, the Triune God has already successfully passed through incarnation, lived a human life, finished His work on the earth, died on the cross, and risen from death, thereby accomplishing redemption. At this time He came back in resurrection; that is, He came back in the success of having passed through various processes. Resurrection is the declaration of His having been processed successfully It was in such a declaration of success that He came back to His disciples. The Gospel of John tells us that He came into the midst of the disciples and breathed into them, saying, "Receive the Holy Spirit" (20:22). After breathing Himself into the disciples in this way He stayed with them for forty days. At the end of these forty days, He spoke to them, saying "Go!" But how would they go? They would go with Him because He had breathed Himself into them. Originally He was the God of creation, but now He had incarnated, passed through human living, death, and resurrection, accomplished redemption, become the Spirit, and breathed Himself into them. As a result, now they would go with Him. But what would they do? They would go to baptize the nations not into water but into the name of the Father, the Son, and the Holy Spirit, that is, into the processed Triune God. Here the Father, the Son, and the Spirit are the processed Triune God.

Before the resurrection of Christ, "the Father, the Son, and the Spirit" had never been mentioned as one name. However, after the resurrection of Christ, as the processed Triune God, He told the disciples to go and baptize all the nations into the name of the Father, the Son, and the Holy Spirit. In eternity past God determined to create, to become flesh, to pass through human living, to be crucified, and to resurrect. This is His economy. Then, after He made His economy, He began to work. First He entered into time as the Creator and created the heavens and the earth. Then He entered into His creature—He was incarnated and born as a man, lived among men for thirty years, and in the last three and a half years accomplished the great work of redemption among men. Following this, He was resurrected to declare victory, to declare that His work had been done. This is the initial accomplishment of God's eternal economy.

Then, He mass-reproduced Himself. First He sent His disciples to preach the gospel to people so that they might see that they were sinful and were far away from God and that they needed to repent, turn to God, and receive God. Then, when someone believed, the disciples would baptize that one into the Triune God. Such a one would immediately become a part of the reproduction of the processed Triune God, a part of the multiplication, increase, duplication, and surplus of the

Triune God. This is the revelation concerning the mystery of the Divine Trinity in Matthew 28.

THE REVELATION OF THE MYSTERY
IN THE GOSPEL OF MATTHEW

On the one hand, the Gospel of Matthew speaks about the gospel of the kingdom, Christ being the King, and the reality, appearance, and manifestation of the kingdom of the heavens, telling us that if we live in this reality today, it will be our reward in the future. On the other hand, Matthew tells us about the Triune God being processed. It reveals that He entered into a virgin's womb and was born as a man to be Jehovah our Savior, God with us. Then He went through death and resurrection and eventually sent His disciples to "go," bringing Him with them, to transmit and dispense Him into all the nations. Whoever would believe into and receive such a transmitting and dispensing One would be baptized into the Triune God—the Father, the Son, and the Spirit. In this way they would become the reproduction, duplication, multiplication, and increase of the Triune God. This is the mystery of the Divine Trinity revealed in the Gospel of Matthew.

CHAPTER NINE

LEARNING OUR SPIRITUAL EXPERIENCES IN THE DISPENSING OF THE DIVINE TRINITY

Concerning the dispensing of the Triune God, there are a few more crucial verses—2 Corinthians 13:14 and Revelation 1:4-5.

THE DISPENSING OF THE TRIUNE GOD VERSUS THE CULTIVATION OF RELIGION

The dispensing of the Triune God is the basic requirement for spiritual experiences We cannot be separated from this dispensing even for a single day. Whenever we stay away from the dispensing of the Triune God, our spiritual experiences are empty and worthless. We have to know that not only Chinese Confucianism has its so-called moral cultivation, but even the other religions in the world such as Hinduism and Buddhism also have their so-called moral cultivation. In religion, self-mortification is a common practice, and moral cultivation is also considered necessary. For this reason, if a Christian pursues so-called spirituality apart from the dispensing of the Triune God, his pursuit is a kind of religious cultivation.

Whether in Buddhism, Hinduism, or Confucianism, the principle of seeking perfection in ethical pursuits is the same: it is the exercise of self-control. On the positive side, this is to control one's emotions and to not do things according to the dictates of one's heart. On the negative side, this is to restrain one's lusts and to not indulge oneself in sinful things. Wang Yang-ming was the most famous one among the moral cultivators of the different schools in China. In the Catholic Church, the most well-known ones were the mystics, including

Madame Guyon, Fènelon, Brother Lawrence, and Thomas à Kempis, who were raised up three hundred years ago and who all had their form of moral cultivation. Among this group of people, Madame Guyon was the most spiritual one; however, if you read her autobiography, you will find that she had a very strong will, within which there was a considerable measure of her own natural element.

OUR SPIRITUAL EXPERIENCES
NOT BEING ACCORDING TO THE FLESH
BUT ACCORDING TO THE SPIRIT

At its inception the Lord's recovery in China was deeply influenced by the mystics, especially in the experience of pursuing spiritual life. In the first thirty years there was much exercise and practice in this matter. Later we found that without the Spirit, that kind of exercise is just like the practice of having strict, ascetic rules in religion. I use the expression "the Spirit," because today the light of revelation is very clear, showing us that the Spirit is the Triune God processed and dispensed into us. The Triune God who has been dispensed into us has an abbreviated title, or we may say a general title—"the Spirit." Paul wrote fourteen Epistles on the divine dispensing of the Divine Trinity in which he concluded that we must walk "by the Spirit" (Gal. 5:16, 25; Rom. 8:4). We should not forget this word: our spiritual experiences are not according to the flesh but according to the Spirit.

In Romans 8:4 the word *spirit* denotes the mingled spirit, that is, our regenerated spirit mingled with the Holy Spirit to be one spirit. In this mingled spirit the main component is the Holy Spirit. Today in the Lord's recovery we all know that this Holy Spirit is the Spirit of Christ, the all-inclusive Spirit, the life-giving Spirit, and at the same time, Christ Himself. He is the ultimate consummation of the Triune God and the ultimate reaching of the Triune God to man. Once He reaches man, He enters into man's spirit to be mingled with man's spirit as one. This is the spirit referred to in Romans 8:4. Today we do not walk according to anything other than such a mingled spirit.

The word *spirit* is not that simple in the Chinese translation.

Around A.D. 700, Christianity spread to China from Persia where it was called Nestorianism. Today there is still a Nestorian tablet with an inscription on it that contains the expression *ching-feng,* which literally means "pure wind," referring to the Holy Spirit. The Persians knew that *pneuma,* the Greek word for *spirit,* could also be rendered as *wind,* so, due to their inadequate knowledge of the Chinese language, they translated it as such. John 3:8 says, "The wind blows where it wills," showing that the Lord also referred to the Holy Spirit as "wind." As a result, the Persians called the Holy Spirit the wind. Today people obtain the "extract" of different substances to use as medication or for nourishment. It is wonderful that in English, "extract" can also be called "spirit." For example, in English, strong alcoholic liquor produced by distillation can be called "spirits."

Our God is so great, so mysterious, so wonderful, and so "extractive," so He had to use a word that is comprehensible to us. Thus, He says that He is Spirit (John 4:24). God as the Spirit today is not the same as the Spirit two thousand years ago. Two thousand years ago, God—who is Spirit—was not yet processed, but today after the resurrection of the Lord Jesus, God as the Spirit has already passed through four major steps—incarnation, human living, crucifixion, and resurrection. Two thousand years ago He had not entered into this process. He only objectively passed through creation. Then over nineteen hundred years ago He Himself became flesh, lived the human life, was crucified, and resurrected to become the life-giving Spirit (1 Cor. 15:45b). God became flesh, was born as a man, and walked on the earth. His name was Jesus; hence, Jesus was God. When He was put to death on the cross, He was still God. When He was buried and resurrected, He was still God. Today, such a One is the life-giving Spirit.

The Spirit is the "wind" in John 3, but in chapter twenty He is referred to as "breath" (v. 22). In the evening on the day of the Lord's resurrection, He breathed the Holy Spirit as the holy breath into the disciples. This is an exceedingly mysterious matter, which has been missed by Christianity. Christianity calls the Holy Spirit the "Holy Ghost," considering Him something objective and vague rather than as a definite person. However, the Bible reveals to us that the Spirit is definite and substantial like "wind" and "breath." This Spirit is the mysterious God.

This mysterious God has been consummated as the Spirit, and this Spirit is just His "extract." Today physicians heal their patients by giving them medicines. Every pill is an "extract," a substance obtained through a refining process. There may be seven or eight elements blended together in one pill: some for killing germs, some for nutrition, and some for strengthening the immune system. Similarly, the One who is mingled with our spirit is the "extract" of God, the "distillation" of God. This One includes everything, so He is called the all-inclusive Spirit. In this Spirit there is divinity, humanity, the experience of human living, the element of crucifixion, and also the element of resurrection. The subject of Romans 8:4, where it speaks of "the spirit," is the all-inclusive Spirit coming to mingle with our spirit to be the mingled spirit. This is really a mystery.

What does it mean to be saved? To be saved means that a person repents, confesses his sins, and receives the Lord Jesus, with the result that the "extract" of God enters into him to regenerate him. Once he is regenerated, he has God's life and God's nature, as well as God's element, that is, God Himself. This God is the Father, the Son, and the Spirit. The entire God, the complete God, enters into man. Henceforth, man should live and walk according to this Spirit. This is why in the Epistles Paul said that we should live, walk, and have our being according to the Spirit. When we walk according to the Spirit, we are victorious, spiritual, and sanctified. When we walk according to the Spirit, we live Christ and express God. When we walk according to the Spirit, we have life, light, holiness, love, and righteousness. When we walk according to the Spirit, we have everything, that is, all positive things. All human virtues and divine characteristics are in this One and are this One. The Spirit is holiness, righteousness, love, life, and light. The Spirit is all-inclusive.

We may not have that many spiritual experiences because we may not have gotten saved very long ago, but I believe that we all have some experiences. Whenever we walk according to the Spirit, there is light within. Whenever we do not live according to the Spirit, especially when we lose our temper and are altogether not in our spirit, we are confused and even become "muddle-headed." For example, when a couple is quarreling, both the husband and the wife may become so furious that they begin to throw dishes and hit their children, creating chaos. At this point they really are muddle-headed and totally in darkness. However, whenever we are according to the Spirit, everything is clear to us. Let us use another example: during our service coordination two people may have an argument. They argue about who is right and who is wrong, and the more they reason, the more they justify themselves. Even after the argument, they are still very angry, thinking that even if they are wrong, they should still be excused and forgiven. But when they calm down and turn to their spirit, each one of them will be clear that it is his own fault. This principle is the same concerning whether we should serve the Lord full-time or have a regular job. The more we analyze, the more confused we are. Once we are according to the Spirit, however, we are crystal clear within.

OUR SPIRITUAL EXPERIENCES NEEDING TO BE IN THE DISPENSING OF THE TRIUNE GOD

The life of Christ in us is altogether a story of the Spirit; it is not a matter of seeking to be perfect through ethical pursuits, and it has nothing to do with the personal cultivation of morality. Several days ago I hurt my back, so I have not been able to move around too much. One day I heard my wife singing a chorus, "Each blow I suffer / Is true gain to me" (*Hymns,* #626). I immediately remembered stanza 1 of that hymn which says, "Olives that have known no pressure / No oil can bestow; / If the grapes escape the winepress, / Cheering wine can never flow." Of course, she was not intentionally singing this to me, but I felt that this hymn is not bad—it is half right and half wrong. Do not think that as soon as you toss something into the winepress, oil and wine will come out. What comes out depends on what you toss in. If you throw stones, coal, or wood into the winepress, you will only get some powder; you will have no way to press out a drop of oil or wine. Hence, in order for oil to be pressed out, the thing that is being pressed must have oil within it. Whether or not each blow is a true gain depends on whether or not we have oil within us.

The disciples of Confucius and Mencius, the Confucianists, do not have oil within them, so no matter how much they are pressed, no oil will come out. But we thank and praise the Lord that we Christians are the fruit of the olive tree. Once we are pressed, a large amount of oil will come out. For the purpose of pressing out the oil, the Lord prepares marriage for us. In fact, marriage is a winepress, and to get married is to get into a winepress. This is not a joke. The difference is that when the unbelievers get into the winepress, nothing comes out except pieces of coal, wood, and stone. Christians, however, have oil in them, so when they are pressed, oil comes out.

It is very sad that in Christianity when people speak about bearing the cross and experiencing the cross, they mostly stress self-improvement and care only for moral cultivation. They forget the matter of the oil and do not care for the inner life. Please remember that all the experiences of our spiritual life must be in the dispensing of the Triune God. If we are not in the dispensing, we are just wood, grass, and stubble. Regardless of how much we are pressed, there will not be any oil but only wood chips and grass clippings. We may be genuinely broken, but what matters is whether or not there is oil. For this reason, we must contact the Triune God continuously and fellowship with Him moment by moment. Therefore, the New Testament tells us that we should pray unceasingly and give thanks in everything (1 Thes. 5:17-18). This means that we have to contact Him unceasingly. To contact the Triune God is to allow Him to add oil into us continually. In Matthew 25 there are ten virgins. The five prudent virgins have oil added into them all the time; that is, they maintain a constant flowing in of oil so that their vessels always have oil (v. 4). From this we see that we must learn to contact the Lord all the time and allow the Triune God to dispense Himself into us moment by moment.

Suppose that the electricity is suddenly interrupted. All

the lights will go out, and all the electrical appliances will stop operating. The Spirit may be likened to electricity. When the Spirit stops flowing, all our spiritual functions come to a halt. Hence, do not pray by yourself and then try to do good by the determination of your own will. This is the way things are done, and must be done, in the realm of self-improvement in Confucianism, but this way is altogether useless in the realm of the spiritual experience of a Christian. The only effective way for us to take is to contact the "electrical source" and the "oil field," so that we will be filled with oil and connected to the current continually. This is to continually contact the Lord so that the dispensing of the Triune God can be carried out in us unceasingly.

THE LEARNING AND EXERCISE NEEDED BY THOSE WHO WORK FOR THE LORD

All those who have studied in school know that whether in high school, junior college, or a university the education provided covers many subjects. Even if you specialize in a certain subject, the school will provide an education that covers multiple lines rather than just a single line. For example, if you major in a foreign language, you still have to study other subjects such as history and Chinese literature. You will also need to receive training in other areas such as physical education, ethics, and character. In the same way, while we are learning to work for the Lord and live for God, we must be equipped in many ways. We must realize that just because we have "passed beyond all earthly bribe" (*Hymns,* #473, stanza 1), this does not mean that we can be full-timers who forget about everything and simply work for the Lord. Instead, we still must learn many things and be equipped in many ways. A person who desires to work for the Lord and live for God must learn many things and be exercised in many aspects.

The first thing you need is to grow in life. Life is a matter of primary importance. Without life, there is no way to live the Christian life, to work for the Lord, or to function in the church. The second thing you need is to be equipped with the truth. The third thing you need is to be built up in character. The fourth thing you need is to exercise to be filled with the

Holy Spirit. The fifth thing is to exercise to fellowship with the Lord moment by moment. Due to their negligence in this matter, many have gotten themselves into trouble. The sixth thing is to walk according to the Spirit. The seventh thing is to consecrate yourselves to the Lord every day. You all need to learn these basic things. Finally, you need to be equipped with languages. In addition, there are two important things which you need to learn: to exercise faith and to exercise to learn to endure suffering.

THE EXERCISE OF FAITH

The exercise of faith is a very fundamental matter. We must see that today our living is entirely contrary to communism. Communism is materialistic, being concerned altogether with material things, whereas we are God-centered, being concerned altogether with spiritual things. To live a life that is altogether centered on God, we need faith, not sight (2 Cor. 5:7). With communism, everything is by sight; with us, everything is by faith. Hence, we must exercise faith.

In Bodily Illnesses

First, we must learn to exercise faith when we are sick. This does not mean that we are superstitious. When we are sick, we still have to see a doctor and take medicine. This is a two-sided matter. For example, every day God sustains us not by signs and wonders but through a normal diet. We should not think that since we trust in God, we can survive without eating, just like the Lord Jesus did when He was tempted by Satan for forty days. This is superstition. On the other hand, we should not think that as long as we eat, we will be healthy and strong and will live long. In fact, even if we eat properly, we may still get sick, even with some fatal illness. Therefore, we must trust in God.

For this reason, even if we have only a cold, we still have to learn to trust in God's healing. We should not seek miracles but should see a doctor and take medicine while also trusting in God. This is not an easy thing. With some, once they go to a doctor and take medicine, they give up their trust in God.

With others, once they believe in God, they become superstitious and would never go to see a doctor. Both are too much.

When Brother Watchman Nee was young, Sister M. E. Barber was the person who gave him the most help. She never went to see a doctor or took medicine in her whole life, so she lived to only around sixty years of age. Even Paul told Timothy, "No longer drink water only, but use a little wine for the sake of your stomach and your frequent illnesses" (1 Tim. 5:23). We cannot say that Paul had little faith. I feel that M. E. Barber was a little bit too much. Otherwise, she could have lived longer and could have been more useful in the Lord's hand. Therefore, for our benefit and the Lord's, we must learn this matter of exercising faith.

In Material Supply

We must learn to exercise faith especially in the matter of material supply. It is true that the church and the saints will follow the Lord's leading to supply us in love; nevertheless, we still have to learn to trust in God. Consider Paul's case. On the one hand, he trusted in God, and God really supplied him. When he was in Thessalonica, the church in Philippi sent people "once and again" to supply his need (Phil. 4:16). When he was working in Corinth, the brothers who came from Macedonia filled up his lack (2 Cor. 11:9). Yet on the other hand, when he was in Corinth, he also worked with his own hands as a tentmaker (Acts 18:3; 1 Cor. 4:12). Moreover, he told the elders in the church in Ephesus, "You yourselves know that these hands have ministered to my needs and to those who are with me" (Acts 20:34). Here we see a two-sided principle: on the one hand, Paul trusted in and received God's supply; on the other hand, he worked with his own hands to meet the needs of himself and his companions. He did not refuse the supply from the saints even though he made tents, nor did he give up his occupation even though he trusted in God completely. This is different from the way of Christianity. Therefore, whether we work by "making tents" to make money for our livelihood, or we serve full-time and receive the supply from the church and the saints, we have to learn to trust in

God, believing that everything is planned by Him and trusting absolutely in His sovereign provision.

Second Corinthians 5:7 tells us that we walk not by appearance or sight but by faith. This is to say that everything is by faith. We should not complain, saying, "Since I have been serving full-time, there has been very little supply." We should not have such murmuring. Whether we receive much support or little support, we have to trust in God. This does not mean, however, that we simply trust in God and stop relying on the love and care of the church and the saints, even to the extent that when someone sends a monetary gift, we return the whole amount. If this is the case, God will not supply us any longer, and there will not be any more manna descending. The saints supply you because they love you, but if you think that they give because they look down on you and therefore you would rather starve than accept their offering, you are too proud. If you are this way, God will let you starve. Since you would not accept anything from others, God would not give you anything either. This is true. So we have to see this two-sided principle.

You should not murmur, saying that since your minimum living expenses require hundreds of dollars and you have received only a few dollars or even less for support (only enough to buy something to drink to quench your thirst), you might as well give that money to someone else. If you have such an attitude, God sees this clearly and may allow you to continue receiving an amount that is only enough to buy something to drink. Therefore, we should learn to have faith and not to murmur, trusting in the Lord's sovereignty and believing that we are in His hands and are living for Him.

Stanza 1 of the Chinese version of *Hymns,* #473 says, "When one refuses all earthly bribe / And comes to live for God, / The boundless riches he receives / Are indescribable." It is said that the writer of this hymn is Catherine Booth-Clibborn, the daughter of the founder of the Salvation Army. After singing this hymn, we should not say, "Where are the 'boundless riches'? This hymn should say 'limited riches.' What good it is to have one dollar? This is not enough even to pay for a bus ticket. A gift of a thousand dollars would be more acceptable." I believe that the author of this hymn might have often received a supply of only several British pence, yet she still had such great faith. Therefore, we must learn to have faith. Do not be proud and say, "I will not rely on the church or on the saints; I will learn to depend on God." To depend on God in the matter of material supply is very practical, because God is truly trustworthy. However, you should act properly and maintain a proper attitude. This requires much learning.

In the Environment

We should exercise faith not only in dealing with our bodily illnesses and for meeting our material needs, but also for dealing with our environment in our service to the Lord. Our environment is changeable and complicated. Regardless of whether or not we are Christians, we cannot live alone, apart from human society. We have relatives, neighbors, and friends, who all are a part of our environment. Suppose that the Lord would exercise His sovereignty and allow our neighbors to be either crazy people or activists, the children in the neighborhood to always quarrel and be very noisy, and the couples to fight continuously. If this were the case, how could we have peace? If we were to move to another location, the environment might be even worse. Sometimes when we hire a nanny to take care of our children, she turns out to be a poor nanny. Then when we change to another one, the new one turns out to be even worse. There is a Chinese colloquial saying: "A soldier goes and a sentry comes"; this means that when the military man leaves he is replaced by a policeman. Regardless of how hard you try, you simply cannot find a good nanny. It seems that all you can find are strange or peculiar ones. This is very interesting.

Actually, in all these situations we have to see the Lord's sovereign authority behind the scene. Instead of blaming the environment, we should believe in God and learn to trust in God's arrangement. On the one hand, we need to believe in God, while on the other hand, we need to deal with the environment by faith. We should not argue or complain. For example, when you get on an airplane, do not fight for a good seat. You need to trust in God and learn to rely on Him in both great things and small things. This is the lesson that we must learn.

In the Service

In your coordination with the brothers and sisters who work with you, you should also exercise faith and not have your own choice. You should not say, "I prefer to coordinate and serve with Brother So-and-so." I can tell you that very often the companion you choose will end up hating you. Today you love him, but he will hate you in the future. It is really strange that none of the companions you choose will work. Therefore, in the matter of coordination you need to learn to leave it in the Lord's hand and trust in the Lord. Take myself as an example. In these many years of serving the Lord I have not chosen any particular person to be my co-worker, nor have I selected any particular one to receive my training. I do not make my own choice as to whom I would work with, nor do I make my own choice as to whom I would train. Throughout all these years the Lord has been arranging everything for me; I just learn to trust in Him and to exercise faith rather than struggling by myself or having my own demands, choices, inclinations, and preferences. Of course, we should also not have any anxiety or worry, but we should believe that whenever we have a particular need, God knows about it. This is faith.

THE EXERCISE AND LEARNING NEEDED
FOR ENDURING SUFFERINGS

. Another thing which all God's serving ones should learn is to exercise to endure sufferings. This is also a most necessary item of the Christian character. This does not mean that we should create or seek out sufferings for ourselves; rather, it means that we should learn to suffer. What is a suffering? Anything that is not according to our desire is a suffering to us. As a northerner, I grew up eating food made from wheat and seldom ate rice. In the fall of 1934 I was invited to work in Ping-Yang, Wenchow, where it was impossible to buy authentic northern steamed bread, even with gold. At that time I had indigestion due to a serious stomach ulcer. This kind of illness is very sensitive to the fall weather. After I arrived in Ping-Yang, the saints served me rice every day. The strangest thing was that the rice that the southerners cooked was dry and hard, unlike the rice that the northerners cooked which was sticky. Even before I ate the rice, I was scared just to look at it, and I wondered how I would be able to digest it. During that time I gave messages two or three times a day, in addition to service meetings. Eventually I had indigestion due to the half-cooked rice, and my body was weakened.

When the saints saw this, they took extra efforts to find someone to make steamed bread for me. At that time I had been eating steamed bread for thirty years, so the first day that I saw the smooth, shining surface of the bread that they brought me, I knew that the inside was still raw and not thoroughly leavened. I dared not say anything because it would have been improper to do so. When the saints served the bread, I just ate it. They said that the bread was the best local bread because it was made by the only person who knew how to make that kind of bread. I just had to eat it. This is what it means to suffer.

Brother Watchman Nee also had a similar story. He was a southerner. He began to labor for the Lord in 1921 around the age of twenty. One time he was invited to work in Hsuchow, in Anhwei Province, north of the Yangtze River. The northerners did not have regular beds. They slept on brick beds warmed by a fire underneath. In order to provide hospitality for Brother Nee, the saints borrowed a bed which had a framework of metal strips without any bedding except a bedsheet. They told Brother Nee, "We borrowed this bed especially for you." Thus, Brother Nee slept on a bed of metal strips, something he had never before experienced.

When we go forth to work for the Lord, we have to learn to commit ourselves to the circumstances. We cannot expect the circumstances to always be accommodating to us and working for us. This is impossible. Some of you will go to different towns and villages for propagation. You do not know what kind of circumstances you will be in, what kind of things you will encounter, and how much financial support you will receive. Everything is an unknown. Therefore, you need to live by faith and learn to suffer. You should arm yourselves with a mind to suffer so that you can be a good soldier of Christ. Peter also exhorted us to follow the Lord with the mind of Christ, a mind to suffer (1 Pet. 4:1). When a real soldier goes to fight at the frontline, the environment is beyond his control. Therefore, he has to get ready in ordinary times by exercising to endure sufferings.

We said earlier that anything that is not according to our desire is a suffering. For example, we may be afraid that others will snore, yet it may happen that the one who sleeps on the same bunk bed with us snores terribly. We should not say that we cannot take it. Instead, we have to exercise. If we have such a mind, it will take us only a week's exercise to be able to fall asleep. If we do not pay attention to a certain thing, we will not suffer because of it, but once we direct our attention to it, we will suffer. Hence, to learn to suffer is to learn not to be mindful of anything.

That time while I was eating the uncooked steamed bread, I was really not able to eat it, but I remembered that the Lord had said, "And into whatever city you enter and they receive you, eat what is set before you" (Luke 10:8). So I prayed to the Lord, "Lord, You said that we should eat what is set before us; now they have set before me something raw, so I should eat it raw." Eventually I ate it. Thank and praise the Lord that my stomach problem was not worsened, although I indeed became thinner. A month later Brother Nee had a conference in Hangchow, so I finished my work and rushed to that conference. When I arrived there the next day, he was speaking on the podium. Once he saw me, he said, "Alas! Brother Witness is as thin as a stick!" Afterward in the next meeting, he shared in the message that co-workers who go out to labor for the Lord should learn to suffer hardships.

We must learn to endure hardships if we intend to work for the Lord. We should not forget that as soldiers we must be ready to go to war, not to attend a feast. As a result, we need to get ourselves prepared. When we go out to spread the gospel, we have to prepare to go to the battlefield to suffer. We have to pave the way for ourselves in every matter. We need to take care of our living quarters and find a way to prepare our meals. In dealing with gospel friends or brothers and sisters we must learn to relate to them on their level. All these things require us to exercise faith and to learn to suffer.

CHAPTER TEN

BEING A LIVING WITNESS OF THE LORD

A BRIEF HISTORY OF
THE LORD'S RECOVERY IN TAIWAN

The center, the focus, of the Lord's leading to us on the island of Taiwan is to gospelize Taiwan. This is not a small thing in the history of Christianity. It has been more than a hundred years since the Presbyterian Church of Scotland brought the gospel to Taiwan in the nineteenth century. According to the statistics of last year, this group, which has a membership of around 120,000, has the greatest number of Christians in Taiwan. The churches in the Lord's recovery have been in Taiwan for only thirty years. We have forty to fifty thousand people and are in second place. The total number of Christians in Taiwan is less than 500,000. Compared with Taiwan's population of 20,000,000, only 2.5% are Christians. This figure is too low, too small, and too poor.

According to my feeling, this is a great shame. After the Lord sent us to Taiwan, by His mercy and grace there was great blessing on our work in the first few years, and within five to six years there was a hundred percent increase and multiplication. In 1949 the number of saints in the Lord's recovery in Taiwan was only about 400. By 1955, however, the number had increased to about 50,000. If we had continued to increase at that rate, Taiwan would have been gospelized a long time ago.

However, at that time, because we went astray slightly by turning our attention to so-called spirituality, it brought in disaster. We invited Brother T. Austin-Sparks, who was renowned for his spirituality at the time, to help us pursue spiritual knowledge. His visit brought in different opinions and led to incidents of dissension among us. From that time on, we lost our one accord and our morale for active propagation. Because of this, our increase was also halted. Affected by this event, I lost the heart to lead the work in Taiwan, so I went to America to have a new start.

When I first arrived in America, my feeling toward that country was pleasant and sweet. Those who are familiar with the history of the Lord's recovery know that although the rate of increase in America in the beginning was not as high as that in Taiwan, it was still quite high. Consider the situation at that time. Since the churches in Taiwan were hesitating, I went to America alone, without any helper or financial support. They were more or less "sitting on the fence," waiting to see whether my ministry was right or whether Brother Austin-Sparks's ministry was right. In that hesitating situation, about eighty percent leaned toward my side, while at least twenty percent leaned toward the other side. I did not do anything about that wait-and-see attitude, except to let things run their course. I just devoted myself to the work in America.

After twenty-two years of endeavoring, not only has there been an increase, but there has also been propagation. As a result, one hundred churches were raised up in North America, and more than one hundred churches were also raised up in Central and South America. In addition, more than one hundred churches were founded in Europe, Africa, and Australia. Hence, the Lord's recovery quickly spread to the four big continents outside of Asia, and more than three hundred churches were raised up. This rate of increase is very high.

Today many elderly saints who are here must be held accountable for having a wait-and-see attitude. Then in 1965, two brothers wrote me personally in all seriousness. In one of their letters they said that no one can deny that the work on the island of Taiwan was raised up by the Lord through me. They also wrote that a situation had appeared in which over eighty co-workers were willing to absolutely follow my leading to do the work; however, there were also several co-workers who seemingly were taking the way of the church and standing on the ground of the church but were actually doing a work of tearing down. Thus, according to their feeling, if these ones were allowed to continue their work among us, all the other co-workers would have no way to go on.

When I received the letter in May that year, I was clear within that the brothers' attitude was the following: since I was the one who built up the work, I had to be the one to clear up the situation, or else they would have no way to go on. At that time I had already promised to visit Brazil. In addition, in the summer there would be the usual big conference for the entire United States followed by the move for propagation. So I replied to the brothers, telling them that I had to wait until September to go back to Taiwan.

In my letter I also told them that previously when I returned to Taiwan, I usually held a general conference first and then met with the co-workers. This time, however, I would meet with all the co-workers of the whole province of Taiwan on the day after my arrival. The first thing I would do would be to make an announcement asking all the dissenting ones to leave the work. I would not "quarantine" them because they had not committed any sin which would require their being separated from the church, but since they had violated the principle of the work, they would not be allowed to participate in the work any longer. Therefore, I would ask them to remove themselves from this work. After receiving my letter and upon knowing that I would shoulder the responsibility, the two brothers were comforted in their hearts.

Eventually, when I attended this co-workers' meeting I opened up right away and said, "In my coming back this time the first thing I will deal with is the dissension brought in through the visit of Brother Austin-Sparks. At the time that the dissension was brought in, I warned the dissenting ones, both privately through some serious conversations and exhortations and publicly in big meetings, telling them that if they intended to stay in this work, they would have to keep the one accord. If they do not want to stay in this work, they could go out to do their own work according to their inner feeling. We all must be gentlemen, sons of God, and sons of light. We should not remain here to do anything that is against our conscience as Christians. However, in these few years, you, the dissenting ones, are still in pretense, even to such an extent that these eighty co-workers are not able to carry out the work. So I ask you, all the dissenting ones, to leave this work." In this way I dealt with the situation.

THE REASON FOR CHANGING THE SYSTEM

Although I had dealt with the situation, I did not entirely pick up the work in Taiwan again. The reason was that the propagation abroad was very rapid, and I could not ignore the great need. However, in my heart I still cared for Taipei, so even though I could not come back once a year, I still came back at least once every two years and tried my best to urge the co-workers on, supporting them from behind and inciting them to do the work. After ten years passed, the brothers consulted with me. They said that the elders and co-workers in Taiwan had been serving for twenty years and asked me to come back to help them make some new arrangements. In response, I asked three brothers to be responsible for raising up a new generation of elders within a few years. It has been ten years since they were charged with this responsibility. I have been concerned about this matter year after year, but ten years have gone by and still nothing has happened. I felt that I could not wait any longer. Therefore, I told the three brothers that since the church needs the administration of the elders, we must perfect a group of elders, build up the administration of the church, and raise up the elders' meeting. Because these things had not been worked out, I decided to come back to have a thorough change of the system.

Thank the Lord that when I came back in 1984, my view had already been broadened. This is due to the fact that, on the one hand, more than three hundred churches had already been raised up, and on the other hand, I had thoroughly observed the situation of the world and its changes and also observed the move and activities of some religious groups. I considered everything according to the truth and our own experience. After reviewing our ways and practices and comparing them with others' methods, I had a clear sketch. We have been in the Lord's recovery sixty years. Apparently we have already left the denominations, but actually the things of the denominations are still in our blood. Therefore, the old things of Christianity gradually and insidiously accumulated in us. In 1984, generally speaking, there was not much difference between us and Christianity. In our Lord's Day meetings we had one man speaking and all the rest listening just like in Christianity. The only difference was that we had higher truths. For this reason I was determined to change the system.

THE PLAN FOR THE EVANGELIZATION OF TAIWAN

The Goal of Changing the System

We were sent by the Lord to come here to Taiwan thirty-six years ago, yet this little island of Taiwan has not been gospelized. This is really a big shame to us. Therefore, the primary goal of changing the system is the evangelization of Taiwan. For this I have designed a plan to evangelize Taiwan which will require five years and two thousand five hundred full-timers.

Our overall plan for the full-time training and our arrangement and economy concerning the full-timers are as follows: the short-term goal in changing the system in the churches is to overthrow the big meetings. In other words, instead of relying on the big meetings, we should build up the gospel, the truth, and the church life in the homes of the saints. Our situation is similar to the situation of a country or a society. The strength of a country or a society depends on the homes of the people. If all the households are strong, the society will be healthy and the country will also be powerful. Therefore, we will no longer focus on big joint-meetings. Instead, we will practice this way to the extent that even our conferences and trainings will not be carried out by relying on the big meetings but on the meetings in the homes.

Second, concerning the truths which the Lord has revealed to us, we must be able to teach them fluently and speak them thoroughly so that they will be wrought into the saints completely. Especially in the past two or three years the Lord's revelation of the truth among us has nearly reached the peak. The whole Bible concludes with the New Jerusalem. Yet since the beginning of the history of Christianity, there have never been so many precious messages released concerning the New Jerusalem as have been released in the Lord's recovery. *God's New Testament Economy* has nineteen messages that give a thorough discussion of the New Jerusalem. Almost every item related to the New Jerusalem has been clearly explained in these nineteen messages.

The truths which the Lord has revealed among us today have nearly reached the peak. These truths, which consummate in the New Jerusalem, are crystallized in the book entitled *God's New Testament Economy.* We are planning to compile all these truths into four volumes in *Truth Lessons,* with one level for each year and four volumes for each level. If all the saints are faithful to attend four years of the truth lessons, all these truths will be stored in them, and they will become persons filled with the truth. They will not only be people of life, life-people, but also people of truth, truth-people. This will fulfill what the apostle Paul said was God's desire—that all men would be saved and come to the full knowledge of the truth (1 Tim. 2:4). Thus, in addition to having life and the light of life, we will have the truth and revelation. This will cause us spontaneously to become a testimony of the Lord Jesus on the earth today (Rev. 1:2).

The Practice of Changing the System

To fulfill such a plan, first we have to build up the home meetings, and second we have to teach the truth. As for the practical carrying out of the increase and propagation, we have to labor in the community. The present situation of the city of Taipei with its community system is truly unprecedented. Throughout several thousand years of the history of the Chinese nation, we have never had this kind of community. This is really "the community of the new age." One community consists of a number of high-rise buildings, with around one to two hundred households in each building. When all these people gather together, the number could be said to be more than a town or a village. It is also extremely easy for us to enter in and preach the gospel. Moreover, according to our observation of the present situation, all the important and high-class citizens are concentrated in the big cities, especially in the communities. So we absolutely should not overlook the propagation in the communities; rather, we must aggressively work on this.

The Move for Gospelizing Each Town and Village

Furthermore, like casting nets, we have to spread the gospel to every town and village. At present there are three hundred eighteen towns in Taiwan, each of which must have a gospel station, that is, a local church. We need to ask the Lord to increase our burden for this matter and take this as the goal of our prayer, that there would be a local church in each of these three hundred eighteen towns. Beginning in 1988 we will proceed with our move of propagation. If the Lord would raise up one thousand full-timers, we would be able to evangelize all the towns within half a year.

The work for the evangelization of Taiwan will require three years of preparation (1984-87). Thus far, it has already been going on for one and a half years. The primary thing that we must do is to call out one thousand people and to train and equip them like soldiers. After three years, in January 1988, when everyone is properly equipped, we will set out on a large scale. I believe that such an amount of time should be adequate for preparation.

The way of our propagation will be to divide the one thousand people into small teams. Each team will consist of ten people, and there will be a total of one hundred teams. If the Lord blesses us financially, we will prepare gospel vans. If our financial support is inadequate, we will at least prepare a few. In places where the transportation is more convenient, we can do without one. When the time comes, these one hundred teams will set out together to one hundred towns and preach the gospel for one month. They will go out two by two to knock on doors and labor to gain people. A month later two people will remain to take care of the new ones while the rest are re-divided to form new teams and go to other towns. In this way, in the first month we will gain a hundred towns, in the second month eighty towns, in the third month sixty-four towns, in the fourth month fifty-one towns, and in the fifth month twenty-three towns. The total will be three hundred eighteen towns. If the Lord gives us only seven hundred people, we will still do the same thing, but the time by which every town will be gospelized will be delayed until late October.

Whether there will be one thousand people or seven hundred, by 1988 the three hundred eighteen towns in the whole island should all be gospelized. Thus, we will not only have churches in all the big cities, but we will also form these three hundred eighteen towns into a church network covering the whole island. Just as throwing a stone into the water creates ripples, at that time we will be able to use these three hundred eighteen towns as centers to reach the surrounding villages. In this way we can spread the gospel to all the villages and reach the goal of gospelizing every village.

Some of the full-timers who come back after the propagation will go and get jobs, while others may continue to serve full-time for the Lord's need. All these people, plus the new incoming full-timers, will go to all the big cities to work in the communities, not for establishing churches but for building up some bases for small meetings. We hope that we will be able to labor to the extent that there will be a base for meetings in every high-rise building.

The Practice for the Preparation

Some among us are practicing to deliver the gospel from house to house on every Wednesday and Friday. If we continue to practice this, at the time of propagation, everyone will be experienced, knowing how to knock on doors, how to contact people, and how to sow the gospel into man's heart. At the same time, we will also produce some timely publications which we will be able to use readily during door-knocking. When the propagation of the villages begins, I believe that we will be able to gain at least ten people a month, or maybe even ten a week. This is absolutely not a dream but something easily attainable.

THE EFFECT OF THE FULL-TIME TRAINING

It is really a great blessing to all the full-time trainees who have just finished their college education and are about to start a new stage in their life to set apart some time to be trained to know the Lord and serve Him. I believe that after they have been nurtured and equipped through the training, whether they stay to serve full-time or go to find employment, there will be no problem. This is because after they have been equipped, they will no longer be common Christians or even ordinary Christians in the Lord's recovery. They will have been trained and equipped, and they will have received the Lord's burden. This will affect their whole life.

I believe that after this kind of equipping, even if the trainees go back to their regular jobs, they will not be the same as ordinary people or even as they were before. Instead, they will be the Lord's living witnesses, full of life and truth. No matter what they do in the future, whether taking care of a family, living, working, or operating a business, they will spontaneously be the Lord's living witnesses. This will be a great success. It will be a great thing if we can produce one to two thousand of this kind of people as the foundation and basis for the island of Taiwan. Not only will they accomplish the great task of the gospelization of Taiwan, but they will also become the backbone of the church life in the Lord's recovery. Consequently, they, along with their families and enterprises, will become a living testimony of the Lord. From this perspective, it is really worthwhile to spend this best time of your life in the full-time training.

However, the full-time training is just the first step for the evangelization of Taiwan. The next thing we have to do is to set the churches in order. Not only should we be well equipped in life and truth, but we should also be proper in our daily dress and conduct. We have to teach the saints that they should not be loose or dress carelessly, whether in the Lord's Day meetings or in ordinary home meetings. We go to meetings to worship the Lord, so we all have to dress properly and conduct ourselves with gravity. We must be a group of special people who not only are the Lord's testimony in truth and life but also are proper in our daily life, personal attire, and in the way we decorate our homes. I hope that once people come into our homes, they will see that we are high-class citizens. They will see that not only the standard of our morality is high but also that the way we dress and conduct ourselves is noble. Not only so, we should also know how to eat healthily and live properly so that we may become top citizens in the country.

The apostles also teach us how to live a proper human living. We must follow the Lord in truth and life in order to live a life that is according to the Lord's requirements. We should not have just the revelation of the truth yet fall short in our living. This is a great charge which requires us to go on step by step.

A WORD OF ENCOURAGEMENT TO THE TRAINEES

Hence, we must learn and practice a few things. First, from now on we have to be equipped with the truth. We must not waste even a single minute, but rather study the Lord's word whenever we have time so that we may know the truth. Second, we have to pursue the growth in life in an absolute way that we may arrive at the measure of the stature of the fullness of Christ and become living witnesses of the Lord, not only by preaching, teaching, or speaking but also by living Christ, so that to us to live is Christ. We should experience being one with the Lord whether in big things or in small things. Instead of being wasteful in the use of our energy, time, and money, we should walk according to the Spirit in using them. Third, we must definitely cultivate our character. This does not refer merely to our personality. We need to build up our character by learning to be accurate in words, genuine in dealing with people, punctual in appointments, precise in work, and well-mannered in the way we respond to others. I hope that we all would apply the matter of having a proper character to our living, our career, and our behavior so that we will learn to be living witnesses of the Lord.

Fourth, we must learn how to meet. Especially now that we are focusing on the small meetings instead of the big meetings, we need to learn to exercise our spirit, to stir up others' spirits, and to give the Spirit the freedom in the meetings in singing, in praying, and in releasing the word. It will be a great loss if we who serve the Lord and testify for the Lord do not know how to meet. This is an extremely important matter. We must learn the principles for meeting. If we learn the secret of meeting, we will have a special reserve for our service to the Lord.

Fifth, we must know how to labor in the communities. This means that we should learn to knock on doors to deliver the gospel to people's homes, to talk to them one on one, and to lead them to salvation. In this way, even if we are not a full-timer, we can still spread the gospel of the Lord.

We must spend time to diligently practice the above five points until they become our specialties. Then we will become not only the high-class citizens of the country but also the backbone of the church. Then we will not only be a group of people with noble personalities and disciplined characters but also people who are useful in the Lord's hand.

FELLOWSHIP CONCERNING
THE PRINCIPLE OF HAVING A JOB

Concerning the matter of holding a job, we all must have the apostle Paul's spirit of tent-making. We should not think about making big money and becoming rich people but simply earn our livelihood so that we can live for the Lord on the earth. If the Lord calls us for a need after we have been working for a few years, we should present ourselves to the Lord right away. Of course, this is not an easy thing. Nevertheless, this must be the principle of our having a job. No matter how hard it is, there is nothing too hard for God. If we have Paul's intention, when the time comes, God will sovereignly arrange everything to allow us to serve Him full-time. If we continue to hold a job, then the Lord may also arrange the way for us to be a testimony for Him on our job. For example, we may have to migrate to Australia, move to Africa to operate a business, or go to South America to establish a factory. But wherever we go, we have to go with a spirit of being full-time to raise up churches or function in the church in that locality. However, all these matters require us to be equipped first. Thus, we need to try our best to equip ourselves whenever possible.

A REMINDER CONCERNING
OUR GOING FORTH FOR PROPAGATION

If we have received excellent perfecting in the new way, we

will spontaneously give people a good impression when we go forth for propagation in every town and village. Then the saved ones will follow our pattern. Rather than paying attention to, or holding on to, the kind of meeting in which one person speaks while all the rest listen, and rather than relying on an individual preacher, they will depend on everyone knocking on doors to visit people from house to house in order to spread the gospel (particularly to their relatives, neighbors, colleagues, and friends). We should not give people any impression of the old way of Christianity; rather, we should let them see the new way, which is altogether new and scriptural. We have to show people that although we are Christians, we are one hundred percent different from Christianity. We are Christians who are truly according to the Bible and not according to the tradition of Christianity. We do not rely on the kind of meeting in which one man speaks and all the rest listen. We also do not necessarily meet in the meeting hall. We can meet in anyone's home. We do not have a headquarters; instead, we have churches in every village. In this way, the gospel of the Lord will spread rapidly. Eventually, all of Taiwan will not only be gospelized but also "truthized" and "churchized." This is the goal of our propagation.

EVERYONE PARTICIPATING IN THE MOVE
OF THE GOSPELIZATION OF TAIWAN

The widespread move of gospelizing, truthizing, and churchizing Taiwan is an unprecedented blessing and even a great act in church history. We will spend five years to gospelize Taiwan and another five years to truthize and churchize Taiwan. Thus, after ten years the whole island will be saturated with the gospel. Every village will have a church, everyone will know the truth, and everyone's living will be a testimony. Such a future is really bright and glorious. I hope that all of us would receive this burden and fellowship with the churches and the saints about this, so that we may all participate in this glorious move. Those who can serve full-time should offer all of their time. Those who cannot serve full-time should do their best to provide financial support.

If we have one thousand full-timers, our monthly support

will be fourteen million (NT$). In addition, there will be other expenditures for the propagation, so the need will be tremendously great. Now we have more than eighty churches in the whole island. There should be some arrangement in the budgets in order to have that much offering each month. For this reason, we have gathered all the elders and co-workers from the entire province to fellowship with them about this burden, hoping that corporately we can share this responsibility and also pray to the Lord for this matter in one accord every day. We should pray, "Lord, may You grant the church one thousand full-timers according to this plan, and may there be no problem financially, so that we may be able to accomplish the goal of gospelizing Taiwan in five years and establishing churches in every village in another five years."

For bigger trainings and conferences in the future, we still have a great need for a bigger meeting hall. Of course, I believe that the overseas churches will also put in their share. Once the big meeting hall in Linkou is finished, it will have two thousand sleeping spaces to meet the need. Not only so, all the churches in the whole island can be divided into four main regions and have blending meetings every season. In the future, after we have gospelized Taiwan and established churches in every village, we will need this kind of blending desperately.

RECEIVING THE BURDEN
TO PRAY TO THE LORD WITH ONE ACCORD

We all have to receive all these things as a great burden and pray before the Lord with singleness of heart. I hope that the churches in Taiwan would be a model, not only of being full of truth and life but also, in terms of our daily living, becoming the noblest organization in the society and in the whole country. All of our homes, our attire, our conduct, and our speech should give people a particular impression and allow them to see the testimony of the church. We need to ask the Lord in one accord for all these things to be fulfilled.

CHAPTER ELEVEN

BECOMING A USEFUL VESSEL IN THE LORD'S HAND

(1)

It is crucial for anyone who is truly saved, loves the Lord, and desires to serve the Lord all his life to know how to become a useful vessel in the Lord's hand. There are a few things that such a one should pay attention to and practice every day for his entire life.

PURSUING THE GROWTH IN LIFE

First of all, we have to pursue the growth in life. Both our salvation and our growth hinge on life. Similarly, being useful in the Lord's hand also hinges on life. Being able to render help to others depends on life, and being fruitful in gospel preaching also depends on life. Take our knocking on doors house by house as an example. We can see that whether or not it is effective hinges entirely on life. It is one thing for a sloppily dressed person to go door-knocking; it is another thing for a well-mannered person to do it. It would be a tremendous thing if the president of a nation were to go door-knocking. Therefore, the value of the same thing varies according to the person who does it. If the apostle Paul were preaching the gospel of forgiveness here today, it would be very weighty. If we were to do it, however, the result would be very different because we are not as advanced in life as Paul was. Therefore, we must pay attention to the pursuit of life and seek to grow in life.

We all know that the growth in life of all living things in nature, such as flowers, grass, trees, and all kinds of animals, is a moment-by-moment and day-by-day matter. The blood circulation in our body, which is the basis of our growth, is continuous and exceedingly fast. Once there was a brother in the church who was a doctor and who opened a gospel clinic next to meeting hall number three in Taipei. He was greatly used by the Lord to lead many to salvation. He told me that even before a person finishes speaking a sentence, his blood has already circulated one time throughout his whole body. A person grows in life day by day, and even when he reaches one hundred years old, he will still be growing. The Bible tells us that the life span of all the patriarchs was very long. For instance, Adam lived to nine hundred thirty years of age. Moreover, the entire time that he was alive, he was growing. Hence, the first thing that you must pay attention to is life. In all the books published by us, the matter spoken of and stressed the most is also life. You must spend time to study two of these books, namely, *The Knowledge of Life* and *The Experience of Life*.

BEING EQUIPPED IN THE TRUTH

Second, according to the Bible, truth goes together with life. Truth is the word of God. It is not our words but the word of the Bible. In John 17 the Lord Jesus prayed to the Father, saying, "Sanctify them in the truth; Your word is truth" (v. 17). The Bible is an extraordinary book. The *Four Books* and *Five Classics,* written by the ancient Chinese sages, may be considered the highest books aside from the Bible in terms of human ethics and morality. According to my evaluation, the philosophies of other countries, such as Egypt, Babylon, and ancient Greece are inferior when compared with the classical writings of Chinese Confusianism. Even so, the *Four Books* and *Five Classics* are not the truth. In this universe only the word of God is truth. For this reason, we should never stop pursuing God's word. Our pursuit should be a daily matter. I dare not say that it is moment-by-moment pursuit, but at least it must be a day-by-day pursuit. You need to pursue the truth every day in order to gain the knowledge of the truth.

The Defects and Influence of Christianity

Christianity has two big defects: first, a negligence with regard to life, and second, a shortage of truth. Christianity in its entirety is a religion with only a limited amount of truth. Those who are known as the fundamentalists have four characteristics: first, they have deep faith in the Bible, believing the literal meaning of the words; second, they believe in the existence of God; third, they believe in the divinity of the Lord Jesus; and fourth, they believe that the death of the Lord Jesus was not merely the death of a martyr but was for redemption. Anyone who lacks any of these four points cannot be considered a fundamentalist. The four major fundamentalist denominations are the Baptists, the Presbyterians, the Methodists, and the Episcopalians. The Episcopalian Church, which is the state church of England, is also called the Anglican Church. Its rituals and organization closely resemble those of the Catholic Church.

The Mistake of the Catholic Church

With regard to the fundamental faith, even the Catholic Church may be considered fundamental because she also believes in the Bible as the word of God, in the existence of God, in the divinity of the Lord Jesus, and in the redemption accomplished by the Lord Jesus. However, she has mixed a large amount of leaven into the three measures of meal, as mentioned in Matthew 13. In this chapter the meal signifies the fundamental truths. Three measures is the amount required for a full meal (Gen. 18:6), signifying that the Catholic Church does not deny any of the fundamental truths but rather acknowledges them all. To this day she is still like this and boasts in this. Nonetheless, she does not know how much leaven, heresies, she has mixed into the three measures of meal. The leavening has been so thorough that even the Lord Jesus said that "the whole was leavened" (Matt. 13:33). She has mixed leaven into all the fundamental truths. I have met many Germans whose specialty is chemistry. They all say that once the meal is leavened, there is no way to remove the leaven from it.

A Brief History of Fundamentalism

Like the Catholic Church, the half-Catholic Episcopalian Church acknowledges the authority of the Bible, the existence of God, the divinity of Christ as the Son of God, and the death of the Lord Jesus for our redemption by the shedding of His blood. However, for the most part the Episcopalians do not see the truths in the Scriptures related to life. Among them, some theologians might have studied this matter a little, but as a whole they do not pay much attention to it. John Nelson Darby, whom we have always respected, was originally a priest in the Anglican Church. After seeing much light at the age of twenty-five, he became one of the founders of the recovery that took place among the Brethren.

The inception of the Presbyterian churches and the Baptist churches was related to the Reformation led by Martin Luther. During the Reformation, Luther was constantly being threatened by the Catholic Church, and his life was always in danger. As a result, he was weakened. At that time the Catholic Church's power was extremely great, and the pope's political authority was greater than that of any of the monarchs. Eventually, some Germanic princes were disgusted with this, so they joined together to fight against the Catholic Church in order to protect Luther, their fellow countryman. Because of their protection, Luther compromised and went along with their action. In the end, the Lutheran denomination, formed by the followers of Luther, became the state church. Later, one after another, the countries in Northern Europe followed suit, resulting in the formation of state churches in countries such as Denmark and Sweden. Until today many German citizens pay a church tax, and the government participates in the administration of the church. In the same way, at his birth every Englishman becomes not only a subject of Great Britain but also a member of the Anglican Church. Hence, due to the mixture of politics and religion, the situation of the state churches is very confusing and has a strong political flavor.

After the establishment of the state churches, Luther still did not leave the practice of the Catholic Church in the matter of baptism by sprinkling. Soon afterward, however, some of the Lord's lovers who emerged from northern Europe studied the Scriptures and saw the truth of baptism. Eventually the Baptist Church was formed. Since its formation, it has evolved into many different denominations today in Europe and America. The strongest group was originally called the "Anabaptists," out of which came the British Baptists. John Bunyan, the author of *The Pilgrim's Progress,* was an important figure in the British Baptist Church. Later the so-called Baptist Church reached America and was divided into the Northern Baptist Church and the Southern Baptist Church. Today the Southern Baptist denomination has thirteen million believers. The Baptists in Taiwan are also generally affiliated with the Southern Baptists.

In the 1700s, John Wesley, his younger brother Charles Wesley, and George Whitefield were among a small group of young men who were outstanding students at Oxford University. They loved the Lord very much, read the Bible diligently, and determined to behave very properly and to strictly adhere to rules of love, honesty, and faith in God. Based upon these rules they formed a society, which later developed into the Methodist denomination. This denomination puts a strong emphasis on methods of behavior and pays much attention to conduct and morality.

Today these four major denominations, the Episcopalians, Baptists, Presbyterians, and Methodists, along with some other smaller denominations and free groups, are the main constituents of fundamental Christianity. All these groups believe in the basic items of fundamentalism. Nevertheless, many of the people in these groups do not have an accurate understanding of the divinity of the Lord Jesus. Instead of saying boldly and directly that the Lord Jesus is God, they say that He is the Son of God. To them there is still a distinction between "the Son of God" and "God." Of course, this involves the truth of the Divine Trinity.

The Error of Reformed Theology

Of all the different schools of fundamental theology, reformed theology, which is related to Luther and Calvin, is the worst. Although reformed theologians acknowledge the four major aspects of fundamentalist truths, the views of many of these theologians are altogether heretical. First, many say that there is no such thing as a millennial kingdom. They think that it is wrong to say that the millennial kingdom will not begin until the Lord Jesus comes back. Instead, they believe that beginning with the spreading of the gospel through the apostles' preaching of the gospel and truth, human society has been gradually reformed. As a result, human society will eventually become a utopia, a world of bliss. This kind of teaching was quite prevailing in the nineteenth century. At that time, Darby took the lead among the Brethren to refute it. Thus, Brethren teaching is in conflict with reformed theology.

Many of the Bible scholars of Europe and America acknowledge that Brethren theology is the top fundamental theology with the most fundamental truths. These are the very truths that we have received. The reformed theology asserts that the Lord Jesus will not come back because human society will be reformed and eventually become a utopia through the spreading of the gospel and the teaching of the truth. They do not acknowledge that the believers have two natures, the new nature and the old nature, an old man and a new man within them. They think that the new man comes out of the improvement of the old man. This way of thinking, eventually leads to not believing in regeneration. Thus, over the years the gap between reformed theology and fundamental theology has become greater and greater.

Although this school of thought was very popular in the nineteenth century, the belief in a so-called utopia was almost completely demolished by the war in Europe that lasted for four years beginning in 1914. From that time onward, this school of thought has declined and, for the most part, been replaced by the study of biblical prophecies concerning the second coming of the Lord Jesus. Nevertheless, despite its decline in Europe, this school of thought still gradually spread to America, especially in the area around Chicago.

Of the two books which attacked and slandered the Lord's recovery in the worst way, one was written by someone who is of the school of reformed theology. The two groups which published these two books were originally one group. After the original group divided into two, one group remained in fundamental theology, not in the high-class fundamental theology, but in the reformed theology. It was this group that put out *The God-Men* to oppose the Lord's recovery. Those who were in the other group did not agree to remain in fundamental theology, so they had another start and founded the Evangelical Orthodox Church. They appointed themselves "bishops" and purchased "bishops' robes." This second group put out *The Mindbinders* to oppose the Lord's recovery.

Fighting the Good Fight of the Truth

This shows us that we should be orthodox, not only related to the fundamental truths but also in the matter of life. We absolutely believe in the matter of regeneration and confess that Christians have two natures—the nature of the new man and the nature of the old man. This is the orthodox truth concerning life. In the matter of truth we have received a great deal of help from the Brethren—in particular, concerning the interpretation of prophecies. G. H. Pember, Robert Govett, and D. M. Panton were very thorough and precise in their studies, always interpreting the Bible according to the accurate meaning of the words. Hardly any mistakes can be found in their works. Based on their interpretations, and standing on their shoulders, we have examined and pursued the truth and have gone on to see deeper things.

On the final day of depositions for the lawsuit against the book *The Mindbenders*, its chief editor and those involved in its publication all capitulated. They had no way to continue debating with the Lord's recovery. Since they could not understand what we were saying, they had no way to fight the battle. In the book *The Four Major Steps of Christ,* I refer to the three successive steps taken by the Triune God in His work and in His move. This refers to something economical, something related to His move. Yet the author of *The Mindbenders* wrongly accused me of saying that there are three successive steps taken by God in His existence. What they did was very subtle.

In terms of the existence of God, we use the term *coexistence*. In God's existence, the Father, the Son, and the Spirit co-exist in the way of coinhering. This is according to the Lord Jesus' speaking: "I am in the Father and the Father is in Me" (John 14:10); "I and the Father who sent Me" (8:16); and "Yet I am not alone, because the Father is with Me" (16:32). We also said clearly that the Father, the Son, and the Spirit co-existed in the Old Testament. In terms of God's move, the Old Testament age was the age of the Father. Nevertheless, the Son and the Spirit were also there. In terms of God's move, it was the Son who moved and was processed. Yet when the Son moved, the Father was with Him. At the same time, the Spirit was also present as the essence within Him and the power upon Him. It was by the Spirit that He cast out demons and preached the gospel. Thus, all three were there. In the Epistles, it is the age of the Spirit, and it is the Spirit who is moving. Yet when the Spirit moves, He moves as the realization of Christ, and He also moves with the Father. Hence, in terms of Their existence and essence, regardless of which age it is, the three of the Divine Trinity always take the way of coexistence and coinherence. In terms of Their move, however, They are in succession: first the Father, then the Son, and then the Spirit.

The reason we initiated the lawsuit was to fight for the reputation of the Lord's recovery. The changes made by the slanderers turned our teaching into the heresy of modalism. I have said repeatedly that we are not modalists. Although we say that the Son is the Father (Isa. 9:6) and that the Son became the Spirit (1 Cor. 15:45b), this is the teaching concerning the Trinity, not the teaching of modalism. In America, some teach modalism while others teach tritheism. But the Lord's recovery is very balanced; we advocate neither modalism nor tritheism but emphasize the Trinity and speak in great detail about the essential Trinity and the economical Trinity. This may be quite new to the average theologian and professor in seminaries in America. In order to get a deeper understanding of this truth, some young brothers purposely have dived into all the theology from the age of the church fathers to the present time and found out all the truths related to the Divine Trinity.

Christianity has already been on the earth for two thousand years. Perhaps one day many of our young people will go to the West, especially to America, for propagation. We know that in America there is a lot of trouble when it comes to truth. It is a place where truth easily gives rise to debate. Therefore, every one of us has to study the truth in depth so that when the time comes, we can show our real aptitude.

Firstly Being Equipped with the Truth

In order to go forth to work for the Lord, first we must equip ourselves that we may be enriched in the knowledge of the truth. If we do this, whenever we speak, we will be able to present the truth clearly and reasonably, and those who hear us will also be convinced. The present world has been polluted by Christianity for more than one thousand years, so the truth of God has no way to spread. Therefore, today we all have to receive the commission to spread the truth throughout the world. This is not an easy thing. It is not like in the past when the Western missionaries came to China. At that time the Chinese people were like blank sheets of paper toward Christianity. The missionaries just hired some poor or low-class people by giving them candy or money. They asked them to cook meals or sweep the floor for them, and then they preached a little sermon to them. But today we cannot do that when we go to South America, Europe, or Africa. Because all these places have already been fully polluted by Christianity, when we go, we must be familiar with the truth and have much learning in the matter of service so that we may be able to meet the need.

As those who serve the Lord we must be equipped in these two matters: the growth in life and the familiarity with the truth. Therefore, we should be diligent not only in reading the Bible, but also in reading the spiritual books. We have to spend time to study every page of every book that has been published from the time of Brother Nee until this day. We have to try our best to make good use of our time, reading a little bit even after every meal. We have to practice this to the extent that we have a book in hand all the time. Even before bedtime, we should study a little more.

If we are willing to spend all our effort, all our heart, and all our time to study the truth, we will be able to lay a very good foundation within two years. In addition, we should learn to serve. Young people have to be trained, either for two years or for four years. During this training period, other than all the required courses, all the spiritual publications must be considered extracurricular reading and be studied with diligence. It is a great loss to miss even one of them. This will help you to be equipped in the truth so that when you go out to preach, you will be very fluent in speaking and able to speak without any difficulty at all. Do not learn the truth only on the surface; rather, learn it to the extent that you not only know how to speak the truth but also how to speak it with great skill.

In order to be familiar with the truth, we must read the Bible thoroughly and read many spiritual books. It is neither a boast nor a deception to say that all the books in the Lord's recovery are the extracts of the truths in Christianity. They are the crystallization of the study of the Bible and the spiritual life-experiences of Christians throughout the last two thousand years. Hence, we should endeavor to enter into all these spiritual riches and not waste our time or money on other unnecessary pursuits. We should save all our time and money in order to spend them on studying the Bible and spiritual books. In this way, after a few years of study we will have a thorough grasp of the truth.

To meet the great need of the Lord's recovery all over the earth, we must cooperate with the Lord's move by observing the outward situation on the one hand and being led by the Lord within on the other. Prior to this, however, we have to be equipped with the truth. This is a very crucial matter.

CHAPTER TWELVE

BECOMING A USEFUL VESSEL IN THE LORD'S HAND

(2)

Besides pursuing the growth in life and being equipped in the truth, as mentioned in the preceding chapter, we also need to build up several other things if we want to be useful vessels in the Lord's hand.

BUILDING UP OUR CHRISTIAN LIVING

Third, we must develop a habit and build up a life of praying every day, fellowshipping with the Lord all the time, confessing our sins to the Lord constantly, and enjoying the infilling of the Holy Spirit at every moment. We must build up these things in our Christian life. Prayer is a daily necessity; it should not be skipped even for one day. This refers not to prayers in the meetings but to prayers in private. Every day we must pray, fellowship with the Lord, and confess our sins, not allowing any barrier to remain between us and the Lord. If we have a negative feeling toward someone who coordinates or serves with us, we do not need to disclose it to him lest we give the devil an opportunity to damage the work. We should, however, still go to the Lord to deal with this matter, saying, "Lord, I have a bad feeling toward him. I am tired of him and do not approve of what he says. Please forgive me and transform me."

In hospitals, doctors and nurses contact all kinds of patients every day and are contaminated by different kinds of germs. The best way for them to be protected is by continually washing their hands. Every time after they contact a patient, they wash their hands so that no germs remain on them. Our confession and repentance must also be like this. In addition, we also need to fellowship with the Lord and receive the infilling of the Holy Spirit constantly. We should not analyze too much in our mind, but we should just practice this every day.

BUILDING UP OUR CHRISTIAN CHARACTER

Fourth, a person who serves the Lord should not be light in speech or loose in behavior. We need to cultivate our human character and disposition in order to build up our Christian character. Do not be frivolous or loose but instead be grave and dignified. This is not simply to give ourselves an air of solemnity but to be sober as is fitting for Christians. The sisters, in particular, should conduct themselves with gravity. It is an unchanging principle that there should be a distinction between males and females. Women should not have any casual physical contact with men, talk with them in a frivolous way, or be so loose as to hold hands with them or put their arm around their shoulders. Sisters, if you do any of these things, you depreciate yourselves. Of course, you may not have any intention to do anything evil, but others will despise your behavior. Similarly, the brothers should not be playful or light. Instead, you should be grave and proper. This is to build up your character. Do not open your mouth if there is no need for you to say anything. If you do say something, however, you should mean what you say. If you say something wrong, confess it right away. Moreover, whenever you say something, you should keep your word. Do everything properly and seriously. If you have an appointment with someone, you should be on time. You should also do whatever you have promised others that you will do, even if it causes you to suffer a loss. If we build up this kind of character, surely we will be weighty.

Two people can do the same thing, but the weightiness of the action does not depend on the action itself, but on the person who is doing it. Therefore, we need to build up our character. This includes our clothing and adornment. The sisters like to adorn their face and hair. The way you comb your hair and present your face reveals what kind of person you are; it depicts your character to the uttermost. Of course, there are no outward laws telling us what to do. I believe, however, that we all understand what Paul meant when he said, "That women adorn themselves in proper clothing with modesty and sobriety" (1 Tim. 2:9). Although it is hard to say what kind of clothing is "proper," all people who are upright, not only Christians but even non-Christians, know the kind of clothing that is considered proper. Even non-Christians, if they are upright, know that clothes that expose the chest and arms are improper and inappropriate.

The purpose of clothing is not only to protect us from the cold, but even more to cover our body. The reason that human beings need to wear clothing is because man sinned and as a result gained a sense of shame toward his nakedness. Originally, man did not have to wear clothes because he did not have sin or know sin and thus did not have the sense of shame. But since the day that sin entered into man due to the fall, man began to have a sense of shame. Thus, man started to feel that it was wrong to be naked and that he needed to be covered. Hence, clothing in the Bible is not primarily for protecting us from the cold but for covering our body to remove our shame of nakedness. Today, however, the clothes that are in fashion all violate this principle. People think that the more they expose their body, the better. Therefore, nearly all of the clothes that are in style are against the principle of morality. There are two ways that the human body can be exposed: one way is to be completely naked and without the covering of any clothes; another way is to be clothed in a way that exposes the shape of one's body. Both are against the biblical principle.

For this reason, we should not find it strange that since the ancient times, people who fear God, whether Jews or Arabs, Catholics or Episcopalians, males or females, priests or nuns, all wear clothes that completely cover their body. This does not mean that all of our clothing has to be old-fashioned and peculiar. Nonetheless, according to the principle, firstly, we should cover our body; secondly, we should not overexpose our figure. This matter has very much to do with our character, our personality, our gravity, and our dignity. We must not forget that we are doing the King's business. We are just like the imperial officials and special envoys. Therefore, when we go to visit people, we must dress properly so that when people look at our clothing and our manner, they cannot but welcome and respect us. Hence, we must cultivate and build up this matter.

The effectiveness of our work and the weightiness of our words all depend on the way we dress ourselves. The Chinese have a saying: "Words from a person of little significance carry little weight." How then can we be people who are weighty instead of being people of little significance? It all depends upon our character, our speech, our appearance, and our clothing and adornment. Suppose we were to wear a strange garment that was very colorful with two red stripes in the front and two yellow stripes on the shoulders. When people saw us, surely they would say that we were probably circus performers. How could they believe that we were preaching Jesus and teaching the truth?

LEARNING LANGUAGES

We may have growth in life, the infilling of the Holy Spirit, fellowship with the Lord without any barrier, a good character, and constitution with truth; however, if we do not have a good command of language, this will be a shortcoming. When I say that we must have a good command of language, I am referring not only to foreign languages but also to our mother tongue. If we intend to speak for the Lord but do not have an adequate vocabulary, even if we have a great deal of knowledge within us, we will not be able to adequately express any of it. If this is the case, then everything that we have learned will be in vain. We often hear people say, "I know a lot, but I do not know how to say it. I really understand this matter, but I do not know how to explain it." It is useless to say this. If you do not know how to say what you know, then whatever you say will be in vain, and even if you try to say something it will be as if you have not said anything. For this reason, we must have much learning with regard to language. The first thing we have to learn is our mother tongue. The Chinese people constitute one-fourth of the world's population, so we must have a good command of the Chinese language so that we may be able to speak for the Lord.

Second, since we have a desire to know the Bible, we must go back to the original language. Therefore, we have to study Greek, the language in which the New Testament was written. We should at least be able to recognize the Greek alphabet, learn some basic grammar, learn to use Greek dictionaries, and read the interlinear Greek-English Bible. In this way, once we read a Greek word, we will recognize it and know how to study it. This will help us in the study of the truth. This is not very difficult, so I hope that we all can learn Greek at least to this extent.

Third, we have to learn English well, since it is today's international language. Wherever we go, it may be all right if we do not know other languages, but if we do not know English, it will be very difficult for us to get around. Even if we go to regions like India, Burma, and Africa, as long as we can speak a little English, we will be able to travel anywhere freely. Therefore, once we know English, we will be able to travel throughout the world. We can be sure that in the future many will be sent to the various parts of the world. Moreover, since Taiwan is a center and base of the Lord's recovery, many saints from different countries all over the world will come to visit. Therefore, we need to learn English all the more.

Furthermore, we have to seek the Lord's leading to learn an extra language, such as Spanish, French, or German. Any additional equipping will give the Lord an additional way in us. Generally speaking, if we want to serve the Lord full-time, we should be familiar with at least four languages.

I predict that in no more than six or seven years, many of our young full-timers will be sent forth, unless they do not have the burden, the environment does not allow it, or they do not have the leading in their spirit. I really hope that the Lord will enable us to carry out our plan, so that within ten years all of Taiwan will be gospelized and will even more be saturated with the truth and the church. The degree of saturation, however, will depend on the number of people who labor. The more laborers, the greater the intensity of saturation will be.

Not to mention other places, the communities in Taiwan alone will require the labor of several hundred people. Suppose that right now we had five hundred full-timers who were devoted to laboring in the communities in Taipei. I believe that they would be able to lead three or five thousand people to salvation in a month. If we have five hundred full-timers coordinating with approximately one thousand eight hundred working saints or elderly saints to knock on doors every day, just consider how great the impact would be!

If there is no longer the need to take care of the towns and villages, all of the full-timers can stay in Taipei to labor in the communities. If we did this, I believe that within a year we may be able to bring in ten thousand people. However, we cannot do this, because it is against the principle of the Bible. The book of Acts shows us that when the number of saved ones in Jerusalem increased, they should have spread out for propagation. However, because they failed to do so, God had to raise up persecution to force them out. We should not wait until God drives us out; rather, we should take the initiative to cooperate with God. In five or six years, when a church has been raised up in every town and when almost every city or village has been evangelized, we should all go abroad. By that time, all of the full-time serving ones will have gained a thorough knowledge of the truth, will have become experienced in the work, and will be able to meet the need in the matter of language. Therefore, they will be able to go abroad immediately for the Lord's work.

Today scattered throughout the five continents there are more than six hundred churches who are waiting. Our going there will simply be a reaction or a response. These churches will welcome us very much. Do not think that there is not any need in America. This is not true. There is a need for us to go even to America. Once we go, we will bring in a kind of mutual flow between us. Then America will be stirred up. The circulation of blood is essential to the health of our body. This is the Lord's ordination. At Paul's time, people could communicate and fellowship with one another only through sailboats or the Roman highways. Today we are in the age of the "Global Village." The whole world is just a big village. We can communicate conveniently through airplanes, telephones, telegrams, computers, television, and radio broadcasts. Thus, we must seize the opportunity to have more fellowship with one another.

Thank the Lord that He has given us three great resources: first, the rich truths; second, the churches scattered all over the globe; and third, a stable political situation, a prosperous economy, and an advanced educational system which enables us to produce a group of young full-time serving ones. Today on this small island of Taiwan twenty million people are gathered here. They are all of high quality and are just like fish for us to catch. Recently, with only a few days of labor we were able to gain more than two hundred people. The educational foundation is the source of this. Moreover, the prosperity of Taiwan's economy makes it possible to meet the needs of the full-timers. All of these situations are the Lord's doing. Hence, we all have to grasp the opportunity to equip ourselves.

LEARNING TO KNOW THE CHURCH

Sixth, we must learn to know the church. Everything we do should be for the church and by the church; we should never be detached from the church. Furthermore, we should be protected, restricted, and led by the church, which includes all the brothers and sisters. In other words, we must learn not to act independently but to coordinate with the brothers and sisters. Coordination is a matter of the church. Even if someone were an all-powerful "giant" who was able to do everything, he still could not be separated from the church. I have been serving the Lord for many years, but to this day I have never been detached from the church. Instead, I always do everything with the church. I would not do anything apart from the church.

We must see that God is one, the Lord is one, Christ is one, redemption is one, salvation is one, the church is one, the work is one, and the testimony is one. Wherever we go, all of these items are one. Those who cause trouble are those who think that they are capable of doing something and who try to accomplish something. Here I want to exhort all of you solemnly that you should never do such a thing. We have to realize that there is only one recovery. If we want to do something different, we are finished. I am not here boasting of my age, but I have traveled throughout the six continents of the earth and have established numerous churches through the ministry that the Lord has given to me. My secret is that I have never been detached from the church. I am not able to accomplish so much by myself. If I were to be separated from the church, I would not be able to establish even three churches, let alone three hundred churches. Therefore, we all have to learn to labor in the church and to work with others.

LIVING A HEALTHY LIFE

Seventh, we need to learn to live a healthy life. Let me give a brief testimony. In my youth I never received guidance on how to live a proper everyday life at home, or on how to eat properly. I never knew what health and nutrition meant. Moreover, due to my hard-working disposition, I frequently went beyond what I could bear. Eventually, in 1943 when I was just thirty years old, I already had a serious stomach ulcer due to my excessive labor. After that, I became seriously ill with tuberculosis. I had ruined my body to such an extent.

As soon as I was sick with tuberculosis, I knew that I needed an extended period of recuperation without disturbance, or else I would die very soon. At that time it was common in China for people to eventually die due to inadequate rest. Therefore, I made a painful decision to put aside all my work and responsibility. After two and a half years of quiet rest, I was fully restored in my body, and in 1946 I was able to stand up and minister again. From that time until now, I have been laboring continually for over forty years without having had any serious illness again.

During the period of my recuperation, I was under the supervision and care of some of the saints from Chefoo who were nurses and doctors. It was through their teaching that I learned a great deal about health. Since then, I have been living according to the knowledge of personal health which I had learned. This is why until today I am still healthy and strong and able to minister here.

I will mention a few simple points here, hoping that all of us will be sure to remember them. While I have not been strictly abiding by all these points in all these forty years, I have been practicing them most of the time, so even until today I am still very healthy. First of all, you should pay attention to your diet. Do not eat or drink carelessly. You should absolutely avoid fatty meat and red meat. Do not say, "I love pork leg with all its fat, so I eat a lot." If you indulge in eating unhealthy food, you are committing gradual suicide. According to my experience, among the different kinds of meat, fish is the best, chicken is next, and then lamb and beef; it is better to avoid pork because it does more harm than good. The Bible can never be wrong. Leviticus prohibits the eating of pork (11:7) because it has no profit. Moreover, try your best to avoid any food that is deep-fried. If you have to eat some, try your best to remove the skin and eat only the meat. Some people especially love to eat the skin of fried chicken. By so doing, they are cutting short their life expectancy. Third, do not eat too many sweet things. Fourth, avoid eating any heavily-seasoned food. Salted food is the worst. While you are still young, learn to eat food without grease and heavy seasoning, and over a period of time you will be accustomed to it.

Furthermore, while you should avoid overeating, you should not allow your stomach to be empty. Do not think that because you are still young, you are strong enough to hold yourself up. Eventually you will fall sick. I am really concerned for a certain brother who loves the Lord. He has been laboring for the Lord faithfully, but because he is overly fatigued, the level of his white blood cells has gone up too high. Now he is in the hospital getting emergency care. Of course, I believe that the Lord will heal him, and we should also pray for him. I mention this as a warning to all of you. Do not think that since you are still young and have inexhaustible energy, you can use it excessively all the time. We must always remember that we are limited.

In addition, be sure to drink sufficient water—at least twelve big glasses every day. Water is for the cleansing of our whole system; taking plenty of fluid keeps our system cleansed all the time. A study which was done in America on the young soldiers who were killed in the Vietnam War found that more than one-third of them had blood vessels that were blocked. This indicates that they did not eat properly and had taken in too much fat, so that even in their twenties and thirties they already had the problem of clogged blood vessels. American foods are very nutritious, yet the probability of Americans having high blood pressure, heart disease, and strokes is also quite high. We should take this as a warning. Therefore, it is good to drink some water after each meal.

In addition, you must have at least half an hour of exercise every day. Any kind of exercise will do. You may practice shadowboxing, or you may jog or walk. Furthermore, there is no need to be so regimented; just let your body move around a little bit. After a meal, spend ten minutes to walk. Walking is in fact the best exercise. I spend at least half an hour walking every day. Whenever I feel uncomfortable, I stand up and take a walk, and after fifteen minutes of walking I feel comfortable again.

In 1948 after Brother Nee resumed his ministry, he gave us some statistics. He said that due to the lack of knowledge about nutrition and due also to the poor living situation, out of the more than twenty co-workers who died at that time, only one was killed by the Communist Party, while ninety percent of the rest died of tuberculosis. Brother Nee said that it was for this reason that he went into the pharmaceutical business, for which he was condemned and opposed so much that he had to stop his ministry. He said that if it was wrong for him to go into business, he was forced to do so because he was just like a widow forced to remarry for the survival of her children. He went into business because he could not bear to see the co-workers dying one by one of malnutrition. As he spoke this word, everyone in the meeting, including himself, wept. Before that time I had never seen Brother Nee shedding tears. In fact, that was also the only time I ever saw him weeping. At that time I was sitting beside him, and I also wept.

We do not have a financial problem in our present situation, especially in Taiwan. However, we should not eat, drink, and enjoy anything as we like simply because we are wealthy. This is to commit gradual suicide. I hope that we could live to be eighty or ninety, even to over a hundred, so that we might be able to see the fulfillment of all that we have fellowshipped today. I wish to live on this earth and witness with my own eyes the truth of the Lord not only being printed into books through our hands, but also being sent through us to every part of the world and prevailing in every place. I absolutely believe that this will hasten the Lord's return because it is through this that the Lord will prepare His bride. I hope that we all can see the manifestation of such a situation.

Finally, for the sake of our physical health, we should not quarrel with people. More cells in your body are killed when you quarrel, argue, or get angry than when you catch a cold. Therefore, remember that you should not get angry about anything or with anybody; in particular, husbands and wives should not be angry with each other. By the Lord's grace, you should receive this kind of exhortation so that you might prolong your days on earth and be more useful in the Lord's hand.

LEARNING TO SPEND MONEY PROPERLY

Finally, we have to learn how to spend our money properly. When I was young, I read an article written by Benjamin Franklin of the United States in which he said that making money is easy and that spending money is hard. At first I did not agree with what he said because I believed that it is very hard to make money but not very hard to spend money. However, after reading through the article, I was deeply touched and greatly benefited. The article says that if a person does not spend his money properly, he will buy himself disaster. Very few people, however, know how to spend their money rightly.

Concerning the matter of financial support for the carrying out of the entire move of the Lord here, the need is extremely great. For example, the needs include the producing of one thousand full-timers, the propagation to the towns and villages, and the building of a big meeting hall. I have told all of you that we are all in the same boat. We must be in one accord and offer as much as we can. Although the full-timers are the object of church support, they should still try their best to be frugal. I have exhorted the elders to do their best to provide adequate care to the full-timers by finding out clearly about their family background, their personal situation, and their health condition. In the same way, I exhort all of you who are full-timers to open up and have fellowship with the elders if you have received too little; on the other hand, if you have received too much, you should learn to give some away to care for the need of the churches and the saints.

Let me give you a little personal testimony. We all know that the Lord is our riches, yet we also love money. In January of 1937, together with some co-workers from the northern part of China, I went to Shanghai to attend Brother Nee's conference in which he released the messages, *Concerning our Missions* (later republished as *The Normal Christian Church Life*—trans.). After the conference I was invited to visit Hangchow and Nanching. While I was holding a conference in Nanching, a brother from Hankow who was attending the conference received a telegram asking him to go home immediately because his wife was seriously ill. Upon hearing the news I was burdened in my spirit to give him some money. However, inwardly I was unwilling to do it. I said to myself as well as to the Lord, "Before I return to Tientsin, I still have to go to Tsinan, Tsingtao, and Chefoo. The money that I have is just enough to cover my traveling expenses. Thus, if I give away some of my money, I will have a lack. Now what shall I do?" Furthermore, I considered the fact that I had neglected the care for my wife and my three children since I had been away from home for several months. I was really in a dilemma.

The Lord, however, would not let me go. Finally when that brother was about to board the car for departure, I gave him three-quarters of the money I had with me. As soon as I gave away the money, I was relaxed and happy, feeling relieved in my spirit. However, I was still concerned about my own immediate expenditures. Then something wonderful happened; right after I saw that brother off, I went back to my lodging place and locked the door. As I was about to retire for the night, suddenly there was a brother knocking on my door. Right away I knew within that it was the Lord's provision. After opening the door, I received an amount which was five or six times more than what I had given away. At that moment I had a real sense of shame and felt that I had really offended the Lord.

That was just the story on my side. Simultaneously, something wonderful also happened in my home in Tientsin. During my absence, my wife with our three children was so impoverished that they were about to run out of food. Since we had learned not to reveal our need, my wife asked the three children to kneel down beside the bed with her, and they prayed to the Lord, telling Him that they would be running out of food the next day. The Lord is truly living and worthy of our trust. Just as she was rising up after she had finished praying and was going to put the children to bed, an elderly sister came. That elderly sister had not had any previous contact with my wife and had not been attending the meetings regularly. Furthermore, she was a Cantonese and spoke only Cantonese, of which my wife could not understand a word. Being very wealthy, she came to my home by car. Upon entering my home, she said a few sentences to my wife which meant: "This is what the Lord has prepared for you." Then she went away, leaving behind a large amount of money. My wife said to my children immediately, "Look at this. We just prayed, and the Lord sent an elderly sister to give us something right away." Later that elderly sister told us that on that night she was reminded of my wife and our three children and suddenly felt so troubled within. Then the Lord said to her, "Send them some money quickly." She asked, "Would it be all right if I went tomorrow?" The Lord said, "No! Go quickly right away."

Brothers and sisters, this is truly my testimony. I was in one kind of situation while I was traveling, and my family was in another situation at home. The Lord took care of all of us. Therefore, we should not worry about our future. Rather, we should believe that we are in His hands and that He will take care of us and sustain us in a practical way. If the support you receive from the church is scanty, do not complain but rather look to the Lord. If the support is plentiful, do not waste it all, but always save some for the Lord's use. When I was in Shanghai, Sister Ruth Lee told me personally that when she and her co-workers were going to take the streetcar, they would count the cost and try to save as much as they could. Sometimes they would rather walk and save the few copper coins for the Lord. I also learned such a lesson. For example, whenever I wrote a letter, I would use an aerogram in order to save a dime or a few pennies. This was the kind of living that the co-workers at that time learned to live. We all need to learn such a lesson.

We should not fear that the Lord will neglect us. Until today I have been receiving more than ten thousand U.S. dollars from the Lord yearly. However, I still try to be as frugal as possible in my living so that I can have more to give away. Sometimes I take care of some needy saints, especially the Chinese co-workers, and sometimes I take care of the needs of the churches for building meeting halls in different places. Therefore, we should not have the notion that since the Lord has given us so much, we are free to spend it all. No! Even if the Lord gives us much more than we need, it is still the Lord's money. Even though the money is in our hands, still it is the Lord's money. Therefore, we have to learn to spend it carefully, trying our best to save as much as possible for the Lord's use.

Our living on the earth is entirely for the Lord. We should not be thinking about trying to significantly raise the quality and standard of our living. Rather, we should live a normal and proper life, being regulated in our daily activities at home, including our eating. When we need to spend, we would spend wisely; when we need to eat, we would eat properly. On the one hand, we should never sacrifice our health for the sake of saving money, for this would be an offense to the Lord. On the other hand, we should not waste even one penny. For the necessities of living, we should spend on the crucial things we need according to the rules of health, eating nutritious food and using suitable things, but we should not spend money for any unnecessary things. Using myself as an example, I still have a suit that I have had for eighteen years and a pair of shoes that I bought in England in 1958, both of which I am still wearing today. We must learn to spend within the appropriate bounds.

What I have said is not a small thing. Rather, this is for the building up of our proper living. Please remember that one day we all will stand before the judgment seat of the Lord to give an account of everything. We will have to explain to Him concerning how we speak, how we spend our money, and how we deal with others. This should serve as a reminder to us that if we really intend to be His witnesses, we should not just speak in a vain way. Rather, we should exercise our conscience so that we will be able to testify for ourselves that we are absolutely walking according to the spirit and doing everything before the Lord.

Therefore, I hope that we would all remember these few matters and apply them in our daily life, practicing every single item. We should not just talk and then not practice. We are different from Christianity. Not only do we acknowledge the truth and endeavor to be built up in the truth so that we have both depth and height, but we should also be right and proper in our practical living. I am convinced that if we practice all these things, we will be those whom the Lord desires and who can be used by Him to send His truth to the whole world, so that the gospel of the kingdom might be spread to the whole inhabited earth (Matt. 24:14) for the discipling of all the nations (28:19).